TAKE CHARGE

The Skills That Drive Professional Success

TAKE CHARGE

The Skills That Drive Professional Success

NORMAN BACAL

ISBN 978-1-988387-21-5 (paperback)
ISBN 978-1-988387-22-2 (epub)

For more information, visit **normanbacal.com**.

Table of Contents

To Sharon

Introduction

Eight months ago, a young lawyer connected with me through social media. "Would you have coffee?" she asked. "I've just opened my own practice and I have so many career questions to sort out."

This is something I do when asked, sometimes in person, and often, virtually.

It turns out Tara[1] had read my first book, *Breakdown*, and was trying to figure out how to apply its lessons, drawn from my career, to her situation as a third-year lawyer. She left our ninety-minute session with lots of advice and promised to get back to me in six months. We've stayed in touch. I'll get to her story and progress later on.

Tara's story is not unique. Over the past five years I've had numerous mentoring sessions with lawyers, accountants, and students across the country—enough to suggest that it was time to organize the advice. Unless you hire a personal coach, which can be expensive, learning how to manage your career is something that no one teaches in a comprehensive way. Developing soft skills and having a strategic approach to your relationships are critical to your success. They were to mine.

Maybe you're a student trying to figure out where to work or how to find a job, or a young professional considering whether you're at the right firm. Maybe you're debating going out on your own, or uncertain about your progression even if you like what you're doing. I have news for you. You're not alone. We're all living in this humungous pool of anxiety over our present and our future.

---

1. In my examples, any reference to a client or professional solely by first name indicates that I've changed the name of the person. In this particular case, by way of exception, Tara's name has not been changed.

Can you survive in a big firm? Are you better suited to a medium-size firm? Will you get enough (or the right) experience in a small firm? Where will the experience be better for you? Did you survive hire-back as a trainee? Were you even able to find a position? Has an unexpected event (like a pandemic) created risk to your job security? Increased your level of fear? Whether you finished top of class, bottom of class, or middle of class, there are many reasons to be anxious.

How do you get clients? How do you keep them in a competitive environment? What skills matter? Who will teach them to you? So many questions when it comes to your future. So little guidance. And so much uncertainty that the path to success may seem mystifying.

But there is no certainty in life. No single road map to the end of the rainbow. The one thing most young professionals do not know, regardless of how book-smart they are, is how to take charge of their future and plan for their success.

You have a choice. You can float along, hoping everything works out; or you can take charge of your future beginning right now. There are tools you need to survive and thrive. This book shows them to you and teaches you how to use them.

Only you can take charge of your career path and do what makes sense for you—not simply what seems *to make sense. Can you afford to wait to get started?*

Many of the examples I provide are directly applicable to law students and lawyers, but the lessons in these chapters apply across the board to anyone who wants to have a successful career in any field.

Your journey begins with the application to professional or business school. So many of the professionals I know fell into their practice through process of elimination: "I couldn't think of anything else to be." Ask a hundred lawyers. Many of them will tell you the same thing. The passionate advocates, the rainmakers, the gifted technicians, the successful business executives—most of us chose law because... well, just because. We had no idea whether we might succeed. There was no one out there telling us how to do it. My first exposure to lawyers came through television characters. I worried I would never be as eloquent as Perry Mason, or, to use more modern examples, as passionate and cutthroat as Harvey Spector or as clever as Saul Goodman. Perhaps I would be no better than Lionel Hutz. I applied anyway.

Like most students when they graduate, I discovered rather quickly and rather harshly that little I had learned in law school would be of practical value to the rest of my entire career. In a 2016 Gallup poll, fewer than one in four American lawyers believed that law school was worth the cost. A stunning *four in five* felt it had not prepared them for work.

In law school I was taught how to research legal questions, how to approach a theoretical problem, and how to think about the law—by professors who were academics. But in my first few weeks on the job at a small Montreal law firm, I couldn't understand the simplest principles of work. Why were some of the lawyers on the phone all the time? How could I actually get a client? It would take me years to find out.

I could handle the legal research and draft an argument, though I still didn't realize that my writing skills, which I thought I'd perfected in law school, were no better than rudimentary, and my negotiation skills, non-existent. When I had to argue my first court motion, I was petrified. I had no idea what room to go to, where to stand, how to address a real judge. Most of all, I was afraid of publicly embarrassing myself.

For the first four or five years a larger question loomed over me. How was I to succeed? How was I to overcome the fear of failure and the discomfort of knowing there was no safety net? At what point would I go from the person who took instructions to the person who gave them? I had no clue. I felt as useless as a lump of clay.

Yet I became one of the leading entertainment lawyers in the country, well known in the world of film finance, representing not only Canadian production companies but many major US studios such as Warner Bros, Sony, and MGM. I sat on the board of directors of Lionsgate, part of the team that pushed the go button on the billion-dollar *Hunger Games* franchise. I turned entrepreneur and leader: builder of a Canadian law firm success story, Heenan Blaikie, a firm that I led as managing partner for sixteen years. I worked with retired prime ministers and Supreme Court justices. When I was at your stage, could I have predicted any of that? Of course not.

How did I manage my rise from obscurity? What skills did I learn along the way? What challenges did I overcome?

I was once uncertain, tentative, even shy. What happened to me and how can it happen to you?

What about others in the profession who have made their way successfully? Were they born smarter or more effective? As you will learn further on, unanimously they will tell you otherwise.

In this book I've tried to distil the lessons I and other legal professionals learned along the way. They come from east and west, represent diverse ethnic and socio-economic backgrounds, and have been on their own unique career paths. Each of them, me included, began as that unformed lump of clay, waiting to be moulded by experience, mentors, and trial and error. We appreciate the value of our law school education, but we each discovered, in our own way, the secrets that shaped our careers.

The world has evolved considerably since I graduated law school. Success appears to be harder now. But it doesn't have to be, at least according to the professionals I have interviewed. The world may be more complex, but the secrets of success are not.

The roadmap

We will begin with two key elements that define the practice of law, regardless of what career track you take: service and sales.

Then we will look at practical survival, beginning with the interview and where you should consider working. You want to be in a place you fit, but how do you figure out where that is?

We will move on to examine the various skills you need to master, beginning with communication, a skill at the root of successful practice. Then we will examine the psychological issues that affect each and every one of us, looking at how they can hold us back or how we can use them to our advantage to propel forward.

Next we will examine what a law firm, large or small, looks like from the inside, what working in-house is all about, and some other career alternatives, examining case studies of various successful professionals, who have carved out fascinating careers despite regional, ethnic, diversity, and socio-economic variances.

We will take a look at a building brick of the profession—the billable hour—and its impact on your life.

Then we will consider the issues that will govern the development of your career. How do you face challenge? How often should you re-examine your career alternatives

What are the basic elements of the practice of law from seeking out prospective clients, to opening files, doing the work, billing and collecting?

I hope the wisdom of the hundreds of legal and business connections I've made and learned from over the years, and the twenty or so professionals who you'll hear from in this book, will provide guidance on the many different ways to manage your career and face the challenges that lie ahead. Ultimately, *you* are in the driver's seat, and your success lies in your hands alone. You'll face numerous crossroads and choices along the way, but as long as you take control of those choices, success will follow.[2] Until the day you retire, there is something to learn from this book. (Heck, I'm retired from practice and still learning!) I hope it will help you understand your own needs and find the path that's right for you.

---

2. In the words of Alan Dershowitz, in his must-read book, *Letters to a Young Lawyer*, "You are a different person [than I am], with your own dreams, backgrounds and priorities." As he suggests, recognize the differences between your experiences, background, and aspirations and those of the people I've interviewed in this book to apply these learnings to your unique situation.

PART I

UNIVERSAL KEYS TO SUCCESS

CHAPTER 1

It's About Service

When you go out for dinner, do you check where the chef went to cooking school? Perhaps the snobbier food critics will do that first, but the rest of us will choose a restaurant based on three factors. Food, service, and atmosphere. That's what we care about. That's what creates reputation and word of mouth. You'll often choose a restaurant because someone you trust has told you that you just have to try it. It's no different for clients' perceptions of professionals.

Clients could not care less where you finished in your class, what school you went to, or whether you won any special prizes. They will never ask you to produce your diplomas. You'll need those credentials to get hired by a prestigious firm, but once you get to work, you'll discover what all those who strive to be their best already know.

> *Clients who return to you time after time care about one thing and one thing only: quality service that delivers results.*

Law school is all about the academics (engineers do a much better job in rounded training[3]). But practice, whether in a firm or in-house with a corporation, begins and ends with service.

A number of years ago my wife and I began taking cruises. I learned an incredible amount about service from those experiences.

---

3. The engineer at the bottom of the class has learned to erect a bridge that won't collapse! The equivalent cannot be said of most other graduating professionals.

From the moment we stepped on board, the service personnel smiled and said hello. The waiters and bartenders looked for ways to go beyond the basics, they checked back to see if we were satisfied, and then they asked what else they could offer. They made us feel important, even within the deliberately relaxed atmosphere—exactly what we're looking for as vacationers. They made us want to return to that setting.

You probably expect your life will involve different skills from those that a waiter or bartender employ. That's why you're deciding or you've decided to become a professional. But if you're going to be a successful rainmaker with more clients than you can manage, or a leading in-house lawyer or executive, you need to learn the secrets of those who work on cruise ships and at the best restaurants, where everything comes down to the quality of your work, service that makes your client feel important, and results that satisfy the client's needs and wants.

Every one of your clients needs to believe that they are the most important person in your life. It's more than a bit of a fiction—they all know that to survive, you have to be serving other clients. But that doesn't mean any of them ever expects to play second fiddle. Think of yourself as a waiter serving multiple tables. Some waiters know exactly what to do and when to do it in order to make each table feel important. Others always seem overwhelmed; they rush past one table, ignoring it completely, and tell another group they will be with them shortly but return ten minutes later.

We all want clients to see us as the professional in control, the one everyone loves. That is the psychological environment we want to create. Easy to say, but how do you execute?

Meet the Perality beast

I'm going to follow with a few guidelines, but first, I must introduce you to Perality, the mythological two-headed-professional-slaying beast.

What are the two heads? Perception is one. Reality is the other. Perality. If you're planning to succeed, then you must learn to appease

Perception or it will eat you up and spit you out. Perception doesn't care one little bit about Reality. It's on its own mission. The value of your service is determined by the client's perception. Never by your reality.

> *It's not about how hard you work or how smart you are,*
> *it's about how the client perceives your service.*
> *It's about managing expectations.*

The easiest way to manage expectations is to set the bar at an attainable level and clear it high. Let's take an example from our restaurant experience. Imagine you place your order and then wait. Despite your signals, the waiter doesn't make eye contact and keeps disappearing to the kitchen, coming back with food for the next table, the one that arrived after you. After fifteen minutes you get up and leave. Not only are you never coming back, you will likely tell ten people about the bad experience.

Roll back the tape. Five minutes out the waiter comes over to you and your dinner companion with two small plates and says, "I'm so sorry, there's been a delay in the kitchen with one of your orders. It's going to be another ten minutes. Here's something on the house to tease your palates." The reality hasn't changed, but your perception has. This story is one you're going to repeat about the service. You may even be inclined to leave a larger than average tip.

I can still remember one of my first clients, Marty. He asked me for a memo that required research. He didn't mention that it was urgent, but wanted to know if it could be done by the following Wednesday. Being young and enthusiastic, I was all over the project. The more work I put into the research, the more complicated it became. New, unanticipated issues kept popping up like critters in a Whac-A-Mole game. Wanting to make the best impression, I did all the extra work required, didn't sleep for two days, and delivered the perfect response—on Thursday. I nailed every issue and I killed myself doing it. The memo was perfect. That was my reality.

I was just one day late. Marty wasn't bothering me to get it to him, so I assumed I could use the extra time. (In some cases the precise time line might not matter.) I was also over budget, but I figured the work was so good and answered so many other problems that Marty was sure to love it.

Marty's blast was so loud it could be heard in the Bay of Fundy. I was wrong on two counts. "In my business," he said, "Wednesday means Wednesday. And don't think I'm rushing to pay any part of your bill." I was crushed. Marty had his own perception (I was late and therefore inattentive to his needs), which had no connection to my reality (hard work and dedication that went unrecognized).

I've had years to figure out what I should have done. Let's turn the clock back to the moment I determined there were more issues than anticipated. Stop working—that should have been my instinct. Pick up the phone and call Marty. Explain that an issue has come up. Explain why it might be important. Revise the budget to look at the issue. Adjust Marty's perception to my reality. Let Marty decide whether he wants the additional work done, why it's in his interest to want it done, and whether he can accept it a day later.

This is going to happen to all of you regularly. Involve the clients in the decision process. Ask *them* to decide whether they want you to look at the issue, and explain the implications if you don't address it. Ask if they want the perfect answer. Point out the additional time delays to get the perfect answer. It's possible they just want a sense of direction to assist with their business or personal strategy. Their reality. You need to find that out. Then let *them* decide.

Now the client is your partner in dealing with the problem—*before* you do the extra work. The power is in the client's hands, the time expectations are set, the budget is reset, and you're a hero.

Yet rather than managing the client's expectations and getting them on board, too many professionals consider it normal practice to get all the work done to the best of their ability, without regard to cost or client involvement. Lawyers, in particular, underestimate how long work will take, or find themselves having to intervene in other client crises. The last thing they want to do is call the client and admit to problems, so they behave like ostriches, then pray for the best. But do they have to rely on divine intervention? Prayer, as you will discover, is not a strategy.

As managing partner I've listened to countless lawyers explain that they needed to give the client a discount because the work proved to be "more complicated than expected." That is code for poor management of client expectations. The Perality creature has eaten those lawyers.

Successful professionals understand that nothing goes according to plan. Promise something for Wednesday and deliver it on Thursday and you're a goat in the client's eyes. Promise for Friday and deliver on Thursday and you're a G.O.A.T. (Greatest of All Time). Perality working for you instead of against you.

Many professionals tend to budget time for projects on a best-case scenario. Whenever possible, assume the worst will happen in your time budget. Build a buffer into your time line. When you deliver quality work early and on budget, you're a hero in your client's eyes. If it becomes apparent that you won't meet the time line, don't panic and close down. Instead, communicate immediately. Either agree to change the scope of the work or extend the deadline.

Though let's not delude ourselves: sometimes deadlines are immovable. In those situations, I have only one piece of advice: sleep is overvalued.

Setting and exceeding expectations that govern Perality is an issue of communication. One would expect lawyers to be excellent communicators because that's what we do for a living. Ironically, when it comes to managing client expectations, lawyers and so many other professionals are poor to horrible communicators.

One more example of Perality at work to drive home the concept, so central to delivering great service and developing trust with a client. My firm represented the president of a television company, who was involved in an ugly fight with one of his producers, Joe, also a shareholder of the company. Joe was expert in getting under our client's skin, a major part of the personality conflict between the two. Joe's lawyers filed a lawsuit claiming he was an oppressed shareholder and asking the court for all kinds of remedies. Our legal position was solid but required long-term patience to wait Joe out. It might take years to get through the courts, and there wasn't much we could do that our litigators felt would succeed in court. In the meantime Joe was showing up at the office every day to produce a television series and driving our client insane with rage. Joe's strategy was working and our client felt powerless. The file reached my managing-partner desk because the client, normally very loyal, was complaining about the most recent bill.

"Your team is asking me to pay and I'm getting nothing in return," he complained to me.

I could have responded that we were giving him our best advice, and that the situation was tough. That he would have to be patient: our reality. The legal reality. In our discussion, the client admitted he was upset that the other side was pushing him around and our lawyers weren't doing enough to stand up for him. He was feeling bullied. His Perality was that we were allowing that to happen to him.

I could see that it was time to align with our client's perception. I suggested to our litigators that we take an aggressive position on an issue that might be wrong in law, but would demonstrate to our client that we were at least as tough as the bullies on the other side. We advised our client that while there was little we could do to the other party as a shareholder, we could do the unexpected and fire him as the producer of the show.

"Can I do that?" he asked incredulously.

"Does it matter?" I asked him. "We need to be strategically unpredictable and unreasonable."

My litigators had told me this was likely to fail in court—their reality—and reluctantly went ahead. Who knew whether a court would uphold the firing? It didn't matter one bit. The key was to get Joe out the door so our client would no longer have to see or hear him. I was correct in assessing that our client immediately felt we had turned the tables, become aggressive, and defended his interests. He perceived we were now the bullies in control. We emerged as heroes. We eventually settled the matter out of court, after which the shareholder officially left the company. Our client swiftly paid all our bills and, to this day, believes I was his champion.

Taking orders

The waiter brings you the steak cooked medium—you were expecting it rare. You're sure you ordered it that way. Who's right? Does it matter? You already know the answer. Maybe if the waiter had confirmed the written-down instructions before leaving the table…

Marty taught me my second lesson as well. He invited me to his office a year later to discuss a corporate reorganization he wanted. I listened carefully, and a few hours later back in my office, I wrote it all down. This time I was going to be on time and on budget.

When Marty saw the work product, he had only one comment. "This was not what I asked you to do." I was certain it was—my reality. Did that matter? Not one iota. His perception was that I was wrong. My ears burned all the way back to the office, and the next day I bought a Hilroy notebook. I was never again going to leave a meeting or conversation without contemporaneous notes, which I subsequently double-checked with all my future clients *before* starting the work. I have four boxes of those notebooks in storage, waiting to be donated to the Perality Hall of Fame.

When you're taking oral instructions, either take notes in the meeting or, shortly afterward make note of the issue you've been asked to look at. In either case, jot off a short memo to the person who commissioned the work, confirming your task.

These are but a few examples of simple steps you can take to improve your service. In the chapters that follow there will be countless other examples, but they all stem from the same root. Clarify the objectives, set expectations that can be met, and when things go off the rail, communicate. Make sure you and the client agree on what the client is prepared to pay for.

Tim Hutzul, SVP and general counsel at Shawcor, puts it this way:

"I can't tell you how many times outside lawyers who have worked for me rushed off to do what they judged to be valuable work, but never bothered to check back with me to make sure I wanted to pay for it. That makes for a lot of unpaid services!"

Perception always trumps reality. How is that consistent with my next piece of advice?

> *Do more than what's expected.*

It doesn't cost a lot to let perception work for you. Every once in a while, my son teaches me a lesson. While he was in his gap semester before college, he waited tables in a neighbourhood restaurant. Four diners had finished the main course and were about to pass on dessert.

"Are you sure you don't want to try the house special?" he asked. "It's a molten chocolate cake that's to die for."

After some hesitation and internal discussion one diner responded for the group. "No thank you. Just coffee."

Five minutes later he showed up with four coffees, four forks, and one platter with a steaming cake and a side order of ice cream.

"On the house," he said. "I couldn't let you leave here without at least trying it."

He told me it cost him $8.50 out of his pay. "But can you believe the tip was 35 percent of the bill?"

Like my son the waiter, doing more than what is expected without an expectation of monetary reward will pay huge dividends to your career in the long run. You'll see more examples of this later.

Initiative

My next piece of advice, based on personal experience:

> *Stop sitting back waiting for something to happen. Take the initiative and seize control.*

For the first four years of my career I took instructions from more senior lawyers. My work-product quality was excellent, yet something was missing. Something intangible. Something I could not put my finger on. Even my direct supervisor couldn't explain it to me. It took my wife to point out that I was not taking initiative. I was doing what was "required" on every file, just as I had done the required amount of work on a university paper or for the bar exams.

I learned through tough experience that simply doing what's required will not get you ahead as a professional. It will leave you indistinguishable. In today's crowded marketplace, as the amount of outsourced work from corporations reduces over time, you need to find ways to stand out.

Doing "your best" will barely keep you in the pack. As a young professional, how do you stand out?

How does that translate to service? Continually ask yourself what could be done that has not yet been asked. Whether you're working for a more senior professional or directly for a client, as you'll see below there are techniques you can follow to show that initiative.

Developing specific expertise

One of my law school lecturers, David Sohmer, advised us all at the beginning of second year to find the narrowest area of law and become the leading expert. "It doesn't matter how narrow the sliver," he said. "You need something to help distinguish yourself from the pack."

Gaining expertise often starts when you cannot answer a question with your research. Or perhaps you can find only an equivocal answer to your question. Or perhaps it's a question the courts are divided on. Maybe the question involves future implications of a new area of technology that you're familiar with. Maybe it involves a new piece of legislation. Or maybe a world-threatening virus breaks out, and a professional athlete in your town decides he won't risk his health to play tonight. Does he have the right to refuse?

Whatever it is, don't overlook the moment. Stake out a position. Write about it. If you can't find a publisher, no worries. Post your answer on LinkedIn. If the issue ties to an industry, call the head of the local business association and offer to publish your piece in their next mailing. Offer to speak about it at their next event. Blog about it. Post a video of yourself speaking about it. You can shoot it with your smartphone on a tripod in your office or at home.

I asked Ken Atlas, one of Montreal's best-known bank finance lawyers, about the importance of expertise. He reminded me that even a footnote can make you famous.

"Early in my career, I wrote a short article on the calculation of interest in commercial agreements. In one of the footnotes I included a sample clause with an example of an interest calculation. That clause somehow found its way into agreements across the country— imitation being the sincerest form of flattery, I guess."

Things worked out better than Ken expected. That article helped make his reputation at a time when he was otherwise unknown outside his firm.

At this point you might be wondering about the connection between developing expertise and delivering great service. So note that the quality of your service will increase along with your expertise and your experience. You need to keep building that expertise to provide increasingly capable service. You want to create an upward spiral. We'll unfurl this in greater detail further on.

- *Expand client base*
- *Build on expertise*
- *Market expertise to gain more clients*
- *Develop expertise*
- *Begin with one client*

The follow-up question

It does not matter how junior you are or how senior you may become, initiative means taking at least one step beyond what you are expected to do. Sometimes it's no more than learning to think like a client, or like the person more senior to you up the line, including the professional who has asked you to do some work.

The lightbulb went off for me after I dealt with a senior partner at Heenan Blaikie. I was a third-year associate. He was the local legend who had become a partner the day after he finished his articles. His hair was prematurely grey, his eyes cold and intimidating. He had asked me to research a couple of questions, and I returned with the answers, confident but nervous. After he heard me out, he asked a couple of follow-up questions. I don't know if he was chagrined that I didn't know the answers, or whether I was projecting my feeling of intimidation. I told him I would have to get back to him.

I was not going to let that happen again. Ever. As I was conducting my second round of research, I asked myself if there were reasonable follow-ups that someone who cared to know more would ask. I could immediately think of two or three. I researched those as well.

When I returned to the partner's office, sure enough, he asked the follow-ups, but this time I was ready with the answers. Over time it became one of my trademarks.

Tim Hutzul tells a similar story about a point of law he was asked to research concerning condos, many years ago. After a few hours of fruitless research, he returned to the partner's office, with no answer and no confidence. As he puts it, "I had my butt handed to me." He returned to his office, worked out a legal theory, then called the city's leading expert in condo law, who had published a book on the subject. When she agreed that Tim had developed an untested theory that may be right, he cited her to the partner. That meeting went "pretty well."

Anticipate the next question and be prepared.

"Luck is what happens when preparation meets opportunity."

This quote was true when Seneca coined it in ancient Rome, and it remains true today. When I developed my expertise in film and television, the Canadian industry was young. In the early 1980s if you said you were an entertainment lawyer, people laughed. It was a big deal if you practised in New York, Hollywood, or London—but not in Montreal or Toronto. By the late 1980s, being associated with the industry was no longer embarrassing; by the mid-90s it was hotter than a discharged pistol: the most lucrative area of legal practice.

If you can find a niche and stay ahead of the curve, luck may well catch up with you. Better yet, you will begin to make your own.

It's not just about smarts—it's about process

This portion of the book is devoted to so many of you young professionals who are bright enough and love doing the work, but are finding your management of time lines is somewhere between poor and disastrous. Alyssa Tomkins is a partner at a litigation boutique in the nation's capital. She came to the law after pursuing a B.Sc. in engineering chemistry. Her parents, both engineers, were disappointed when she announced she was going to law school, and she tells me that even on the day she advised her mother that she'd obtained a prestigious clerking position in the federal court, "Mom asked if there was still a chance I might want to become an engineer."

The key skills engineers learn include basic technical proficiency and process management. These skills were essential to her first few years as a young litigator.

"When I arrived in Toronto on a big litigation case," she says, "the senior litigator brought me as second chair, not because I was smart, but because I was indispensable to him. I knew where every document in his file was located and I had immediate access."

"Imagine," she tells me, "some of my junior lawyers know how to draft, but they have enormous difficulties meeting filing deadlines on court materials. They have no idea how to move files forward. They can write a great paragraph, but they have no clue how to get a book of documents prepared, printed, and filed with the court by a five p.m. deadline. How can they advance if I can't rely on them to handle something so basic? But they freeze with a project that requires breaking the process into pieces, establishing time lines, and meeting them."

Perhaps it's her engineering background that allows Alyssa to see it all so simply. "It doesn't take much tech savvy to learn how to use Microsoft Project Manager, plug in the requirements, and build a time line. Yet that seems beyond the reach of so many lawyers who have made their way through school avoiding technology."

She closes the subject with some words of advice:

"We spend so much time learning how to write a better paragraph, but not nearly enough time learning how to deliver it on time."

These are but a few examples of simple steps to take in improving your service. In the chapters that follow there will be countless other examples, but they all stem from the same root. Clarify the objectives, set expectations that can be met, and when things go off the rail, communicate.

Still skeptical about your own ability to succeed? The person you are today isn't yet equipped with the tools to succeed. You will see from the many case histories to follow that if you allow yourself to be changed by professional life experience and by success and failure, and if you can see risk as a friend and failure as a challenge, then you will evolve. You will change. You will become one of us who have clawed our way to success as each of us defines it. In the coming chapters I will show you the building blocks and then the psychological factors that can propel you forward, factors triggered by the exact same stimuli that can otherwise hold you up and paralyze you if you let them.

CHAPTER 2

Getting and Growing Clients Is about Sales

You might have headed toward a profession thinking you don't have entrepreneurial blood, that you can't sell, and that somehow, in this profession, you can succeed without sales skills; that you can get by with your brains. If the notion of selling makes you uneasy, you're not alone. That was once me. I had a lot to learn!

The simple truth is that we are always selling, especially in the professions. Every encounter you have is based on marketing a single product—yourself. Your success depends on building confidence in your ideas and your ability to express them. Selling is all about communicating and overcoming resistance. In many respects, sales and service are so intertwined, you can't tell them apart.

Selling can be broken into two basic components: understanding the value proposition of the goods for the consumer, and communicating it in a way that breaks down consumer resistance. In your case the value proposition is what you have to offer a client, a more senior lawyer or professional, a judge, or the party on the other side of a negotiation, to give a few examples. As lawyers, we spend our lives communicating what we have to offer. As you'll see from the numerous examples that follow in this book, the best lawyers have figured out and will be sharing what you're going to be learning.

Whether it's discussing a proposition one on one, defending a memo prepared for someone more senior, walking into court for the first time to present a motion before a judge or a master, or doing a lunchtime presentation to a group on some area you've researched, you need to develop confidence to speak. To get up on your feet and convince. To overcome the fear of being challenged publicly.

It's not enough to have the answers in your head or even on paper. You must project a confidence that your arguments are correct so that clients believe you know what you're doing, and also develop confidence to overcome resistance to your ideas.

School is *not* going to teach you how to project your confidence or even how to find it.

My story: How learning to sell began to change me

At the end of third year law school in Montreal, I was newly married and broke, and no legal firm would hire me. I had to get a *real* summer job to supplement my wife's apprentice salary (she was training to become a chartered accountant), so we could eat more than peanut butter and KD. Desperate, I answered a classified ad shortly after my last exam. I had to demonstrate a brand-new product and would be paid for each successful presentation. According to the ad there was "no selling involved." Perfect, I thought. I had no idea that "no selling" was code for "unless you want to get paid."

After three days of training, I loaded the trunk of my pale blue 1978 Honda Civic with a brand new Filter Queen vacuum cleaner (which I had to sell to someone) and a load of steak knives (the surprise customer gift) and drove out to my first appointment. I was not only selling...I was selling in the French language. Not my forte. Exactly what I did not want to do. But I did need to eat.

I was trained by some of the most gregarious salesmen in the east end of the city. I learned a few principles of selling. I call them my "Alfred Rules," named for the mentor who taught me.

First, never go out on a sales call until you're convinced that your product is the best—otherwise why waste the customer's time? Second, you must be enthusiastic about selling yourself. Alfred's salesmen, who spoke little English, met every morning before going out to sell, exhorting one another to PUMP, PUMP, PUMP at the top of their lungs. We raced to our cars, excited to face the first appointment of the day. You need that enthusiasm to face up to resistance and overcome it. Finally, never ask a customer whether they want to buy; instead ask how they want to pay. After all, by the end of your presentation, you've convinced them of your product and your enthusiasm for it. How can they go on living without it? That's the question you don't need to ask!

The more important thing I learned is that a successful day was defined by selling as few as one machine. That meant facing rejection eight times a day. This was the first time in my life that I had to face that level of rejection. Over and over. I quickly learned to celebrate the victories and learn from the failures. More on that later.

It wasn't until a number of years later that I finally appreciated that this summer experience changed my life. I'm not advocating that you go out and sell appliances or knives (though I have to admit it really helped me), but there are things you should be doing to improve your presentation skills.

Presenting your ideas effectively

If you don't regularly speak on your feet, or if you feel shy or anxious, take an effective-speaking class. That will help you learn techniques to present ideas. Many of us need to get over our fears of public speaking in a safe group setting among people who share that fear.

If you don't have the time or the inclination, there are some presentation skills you can learn when it comes to speaking to a crowd, whether it's two people or two hundred. We'll look at those techniques in Chapter 5.

This next suggestion might surprise you: Take an acting class. Learn how to project the inner enthusiasm lying beneath your surface, which you will need to unleash periodically.

Performers talk about the four *P*s of acting:

- **Process**: Every time you perform, you learn a little about yourself. How well do you tell a story? Are you wooden on your feet or are you able to be spontaneous?

- **Practice**: Have you noticed that when you tell a story among friends, each time you tell it, the emphasis may change a little? And you don't worry that you might be exaggerating. In a relaxed setting you don't focus on the individual words, you just tell your story. By practising your delivery in a relaxed way, you'll become more natural. Less wooden.

- **Patience**: When you stumble, remind yourself that every skill you've learned took patience to develop. Stumbling is a good thing! It's part of the process of learning any skill.

- **Persevere**: You will stumble. You will fall. You will get up. You will keep going. You will climb that wall—the wall of self-doubt. You will improve.

These four *P*s don't just apply to acting. They reappear in the subtext of every lesson you take from this book.

Confidence in yourself is the most important asset you need to cultivate to enjoy a successful career. The sooner you begin improving your confidence in yourself, the sooner you will begin to move forward. You will find these techniques laid out in Chapter 5.

How sales and service tie together

Aarondeep (Aaron) Bains is an associate in the capital markets and venture finance group at Aird & Berlis in Toronto. He was recently voted in a *Canadian Lawyer* magazine poll among the "Top 25 Most Influential Lawyers of 2020" in Canada, in the "Young Influencers" category.

While he always knew he was destined to become a lawyer, he learned the key lessons about the connection with sales and service while working for years in his father's family's restaurant in Surrey, BC.

"Imagine that in the morning we were selling something as simple as a plate of eggs," he tells me, to open our interview. "The lessons I learned selling and serving a fourteen-dollar breakfast plate to customers taught me everything I needed to know about the customer experience, and my job in making it an experience they would want to repeat over and over. I have discovered that those skills are often more important to me than formal legal knowledge, which can be found by anyone online or in books." Aaron lives by the key thesis of this book:

The combination of service and sales will make you remarkable.

Marketing through social media

We can't leave this chapter without an introductory discussion of the impact of social media on your marketing. As we saw earlier, improving your service offering is tied to developing expertise. As your expertise in any area expands, you need to be marketing, and the most accessible way to do that is through social media.

Perhaps you're skeptical about becoming known as "the expert" when there are so many more senior people out there. You have one enormous advantage over all the boomers: your vast social media skills. Use them to advantage. Remember, you're light years ahead of the older generation. Get your message out there. Begin Facebook Live or LinkedIn Live blogs to start groups. It doesn't matter how small your audience is. Use every tool at your disposal to turn up on search engines. If you're in it for the long game, the goal is to send your message of particular expertise out into the universe.

As you'll see further on, mastering technology has evolved from a luxury to a necessity to advance any career. I see it myself daily as an author. The use of multiple social media platforms to expand my network has become essential. Mastering video technology to get out my messaging is something I'm working on. You might perceive those skills as less important for professionals. That's not the reality. New platforms emerge regularly and inevitably, and to succeed you must learn to become comfortable in that environment.

Follow professionals with followings. Observe how they're sending out their messages to their audiences. Begin experimenting early. Drive yourself to stay ahead of that technology curve as it continues to evolve. If I can learn it (albeit slowly at my age and stage), so can you.

As you build a body of specialized work, through the network that you build you'll create the opportunities to get lucky. If you're looking for a particular example of a young professional who's done just that, see the case study on Tara Vasdani in Chapter 11.

CHAPTER 3

The Interview

Before you can sell yourself, your services, or the services of your team,[4] you need to find employment. Whether it is the on-campus-interview (OCI) process, an articling interview, or a new job on your career path, you need to master the art of the interview—the consummate act of selling yourself.

The interview process requires the same prep as a final exam, the same level of adrenaline, the same confidence, and the same moxie that will have you calming yourself when the first question poses an unfamiliar problem. When you need to take a step back and re-evaluate, then call on your wit and talent to get you through. The interview is the one place where you cannot falter or show fear. It's a test! You're good at tests. That's what got you this far. Don't overthink it.

Many students and young professionals believe that a job interview is about presenting an honest picture of themselves. I used to believe that too—until I was passed over in all of my articling interviews. My excellent grades, dedicated work ethic, loyalty, groomed appearance, and calm personality were not working for me.[5] Twelve interviews—zero offers. That's a lot of rejection!

---

4. Remember that the waiter is no more than the front-of-house representative of an entire team working behind the scenes. As a professional you must understand that you offer not only your skills, but those of countless others who support you.

5. One law school professor advised us that the best way to stand out was to show up to the interview in jeans and a T-shirt. Of course, he was tenured and never spent a day in his life trying to get a client or getting another job! He was retained from time to time on appeal cases where he wore a gown (perhaps covering up his jeans and T-shirt).

Projecting enthusiasm

Selling yourself is critical to the success of your entire career. Remember the two basic components of sales: understanding the value proposition of the goods or service for the consumer, and communicating to break down consumer resistance.

The interview is all about selling you as a product to a very choosy buyer.[6] How do you communicate that value proposition? How do you determine the resistance? Then how do you break it down?

Your elevator speech

In his book *True Fit: How to Find the Right Job by Being You* (it's short, to the point, and a worthwhile investment), Jim Beqaj provides a whole new approach to interviewing. Jim was the president of CIBC Wood Gundy, went on to run capital markets at BMO, and was responsible for recruiting thousands of candidates at all levels.

"Before you go job hunting," Jim instructs, "you're better off deciding who you are, what are your values, what is important to you."

Some call it the "elevator speech" about yourself. Jim calls it the "sixty-second infomercial." Before you interview, sit down and take note of the key positive attributes of your personality. Who are you? Additionally, what are you looking for in a work environment? What kind of place is best for you to fit in and thrive? Learn your speech cold until you know it to be true and can be confident in it.

> *Understand who you are, what you want, and what makes you tick so you can explain it in sixty seconds.*

---

6. I haven't dealt with the cover letter that you send out to firms to solicit the interview. That letter must be perfect. If it contains even one grammatical, typographical, or punctuation error, that's grounds for your application to end up in the reject pile. Read and reread, then have a third party read it to make sure it is prefect…make that "perfect."

Easy to say, but how does it work in practice? How do you prepare? Jim suggests you start with the following questions.

- What is it that you're really good at? Prepare examples that tie into a work environment. Real stories make all the difference.

- Make a list of people you've met in your life, teachers and people you've worked with, who share common core values and common traits you've learned from. When being interviewed, refer to them (and their characteristics) as people you connect with well.

- How do you resolve conflicts? If you're competitive and join a firm where people you work with avoid conflict or are overly accommodating, then they may consider you selfish. But if you go to a competitive workplace where people butt heads and move on, they will welcome you with open arms.

- What is your perfect work day? Does it involve any or some of the following: lengthy research, tasks on tight deadlines, sales (if you have experience), working independently, being part of a work team, supervising others?[7]

You're reading this and thinking to yourself, "But if I'm too honest about who I am, they may rule me out as not fitting with their culture." There is no *right* culture. There is only the one that suits you.

> *If you try to fit yourself into a culture that doesn't suit you, you are destined to be unhappy.*

---

7. For the litigators among you, does it involve examining witnesses, writing factums, wearing barristers' gowns, arguing, or negotiating?

Do you want to spend a few years failing to adjust, or accept that it's better not to be wasting years at a place that's a dead end because you never fit?[8]

How to reveal yourself

Here is one version of my current sixty-second infomercial. The one that would never get me hired.

"I was a leading film finance lawyer for twenty-five years and a very good tax lawyer to boot. I also ran a law firm for sixteen years and managed hundreds of lawyers. I've been very fortunate in life. Pressure doesn't bother me. I work as hard as I need to get the job done. I'm loyal. I love to write and I've published a couple of books. Working on two more. I've been studying karate for twenty years, so I'm very dedicated to whatever I take on. People tell me I give a moving speech. I've been married for over forty years. If you were to hire me, I will do my best.

Now, do you have any questions?"

It's all true—yet uninspiring. I would not hire me. Press the buzzer and let the trap door open beneath my chair. Next candidate…. I'd have a better shot opening my presentation with a picture of my golden doodle, Lexy, when she was a puppy. That one always gets the emotions going.

So how is it done?

Let's see how different that pathetic pitch is from the following:

"Since I was a kid, I've loved puzzles, particularly math and logic problems. The more complicated the better. I love taking something intricate and breaking it down into components that can be solved. I get pleasure spending weeks to get a result, even if I make a hundred

---

8. As you'll see further on, some experts suggest you do just that if you want training in the "big-firm" environment and intend to spend no more than a few years getting the best experience in the toughest conditions. Are you prepared to make that kind of sacrifice for your future?

mistakes in the process. I see every roadblock as a hurdle to overcome. Perhaps that explains why I succeeded in my career in film finance, which presented endless hurdles.

"It's that tenacity that has allowed me to publish a memoir, which was a bestseller, followed by a novel: the challenge of my life. Tougher than learning karate. At age fifty-seven I began a second career and had to learn it all from scratch. I guess I excel at taking on new challenges.

"My perfect day is a morning devoted exclusively to my writing. I focus and dig in deep. My light-bulb moments come when I am completely immersed in a project, when I look down at a revelation from a character who's taken on a life of their own and tell myself, "I had no idea!"

"If you hand me a microphone, I can address any size group, without anxiety—something I've spent hundreds of hours working on over the course of years. I was a poor public speaker to start, but I learned that with practice I can succeed at almost anything. My speaking hero is Joel Osteen, and I've carefully studied him and other preachers to learn how to sway a crowd.

"I prefer to negotiate a problem than to confront it aggressively, though I rarely back down when I believe I'm right. Some people believe I can be stubborn, but I'm open to being convinced that I may be wrong.

"I thrived in work environments where I was able to take advantage of my speaking, leadership, and mentorship skills. Managing lawyers for sixteen years has thickened my skin, so I can take criticism, constructive or otherwise, fairly well. In those years I had to learn to acknowledge my mistakes and take responsibility.

"If after hearing all this you don't understand what I can offer you, then we'd best not waste your time. I'm not the right person for you."

Perhaps that was closer to two minutes than one, but you get the point. I want to be working with people who hear my message and gravitate toward it.

Practice

Like any other experience, interviewing improves with directed practice. Just "being yourself" does not make you a better athlete, actor, dancer, or gymnast. You practise these skills, either with coaches or with others who are not shy to tell you when you suck. Try a few mock interviews with friends or colleagues. Have them rate you. Set up your smartphone camera and record yourself. Prepare your elevator speeches, then record and play them back. Are you impressed or indifferent? Excited or bored? Listen to criticism and learn from it.

Work on your physical presence. Do you stand tall and straight, or do you begin to slouch when you relax? You may feel relaxed, but your interviewer can perceive it as disinterest. Do you cross your arms in front of your chest when you're standing? Some misread that as aggression. Do you fidget with your fingers or jiggle your legs as a nervous habit? Seek to project a relaxed, confident, and upbeat version of yourself.

> *Practise, record, critically review, re-record, improve.*

First impressions

Later in my career, when I had the privilege of sitting on the other side of the interview table, I observed that first impressions are rarely shaken or changed. It's hard to recover from a bad or uninspired beginning. The way you sell yourself at an interview is not unlike how you sell vacuum cleaners. Dr. Andrea Wojnicki is a specialist in consumer psychology and communication who trained at the Harvard Business School, and a former faculty member of the University of Toronto. She referred me to research showing that first impressions are made in as little as a tenth of a second. Once made, they're difficult to shake. Unfair? Yes. Human nature? Yes.

We all swear that we will not judge people by their facial expressions before we get to know them, yet almost all of us do it. As you might expect, our first impressions are often incorrect. For example, the science suggests that we are judged on whether our facial features are symmetrical, and whether our "natural look" includes low eyebrows, narrowed eyes, or downturned mouths, which might suggest we are naturally angry people. Or you may have a feature that reminds an interviewer of their grumpy uncle or their kindly aunt.

If you want more insight, consider how people react to photos of kittens and puppies.

I mentored a young lawyer last year. Jacob still has nightmares about his OCI experience. I asked him to pitch me so that I could understand what he was up against. Jacob presented to me as a flat line and completely without passion. I had no idea if he would work hard, if he would embrace the values of my organization, or if he would just come along for the ride.

All interviewers wonder: Are you looking for a job for a couple of years to get to the next career change? How will you manage a meeting or a difficult client? How will you fit on a team? If you're applying for an in-house position, will you be able to convince the reluctant business people in the organization to take your advice? Might you be capable of leading one day? These are my inner concerns as an interviewer. There was no way I could discern these facts about Jacob.

"I'm someone who always gets the work done," Jacob told me.

"I'm fiercely loyal, and I just know I would be a good addition to any organization." And yet he could barely manage a spark of anger or emote frustration at his situation. Is there a human being in there, Jacob? I wonder. Perhaps that's what my interviewers used to think about me.

The problem is that Jacob does not radiate an ounce of enthusiasm. Is he boring or just quiet? I have to guess. I asked him whether he made use of examples of his loyalty in the interview. He said he considered them private. He presented himself as a possibly solid candidate, but no flash. No eagerness.

How would that translate to the workplace? Most interviewers were left wondering. Jacob knew the answer, but his personality could not communicate it. He was a consistent fail by the end of the second round of interviews. The story sounded familiar. That's about where I began to peter out in my own early interview experiences.

Jacob was particularly upset about what he calls "the cheerleader types," who didn't score as well as he did in law school, yet walked away with offers from most of the big firms.

> *We're all dealt different talents. You have to make the best of your hand.*

Unless you're an "out on the edge" extrovert, you'll find it challenging to project the wonderful inner you to others. Your core values, drive, skills, and personality may make you an incredible person, but communicating that personality is a challenge in the interview world of snap decisions and first impressions.

The introvert runs the risk of being passed over. Interviewers are looking for enthusiasm, but the instinct to conform can make us hide that side of us so well, others may think that it may not exist.

The irony is that many of us are various shades of introvert.[9]

So how do we approach an interview in a way that's true to ourselves and to our values, yet leave having made an impression?

Demonstrate passion

One trick I have learned is to focus on stories about you that reveal excitement. For example, when asked about hobbies listed on your résumé, don't simply answer, "I like to ski." Instead tell a story about

---

9. Susan Cain shares some fascinating research about introverts in her 2012 book *Quiet: The Power of Introverts in a World That Can't Stop Talking.*

the craziest ski run of your life. How you had to survive the black diamond run that you accidentally took as a novice. Narratives animate life and will animate your interview responses.

This technique is particularly important when you are being interviewed by a group. You can either allow yourself to be intimidated by the questions fired from all directions, or you can turn the situation to your favour. It's much easier to connect one of your exuberant stories to the person in the room who is the skier, or the artist, or the one who loves to read murder mysteries, like you do. And you find out those things by asking your own questions to the interviewers.

> *Interview the interviewers.*

Connect through your passion with one of the interviewers and turn it into a conversation about your shared interest. Everyone in the room will notice.

If your passion is reading fiction, when the inevitable open-ended comment arises, "I see you like to read," don't simply nod your head. Have your story ready about a passage from your favourite author that reveals something about who you are and how you connect to it. Ask the interviewer about her favourite author. See if you can find some common ground, or ask for a book recommendation. That is how you reveal character. That makes you memorable.

As you expand your material for what comes after the first sixty seconds, weave those moments and your inventory of exciting stories into your presentation. Learn from the great litigators, who will tell you that the narrative sells judges and juries. This is how you project that "private you" into your interviews. Maybe it's a story about your most exciting life experience, the feeling at the top of a difficult mountain you climbed, or the challenges you overcame on the road to this point in your life. Focus on the drama and the humour. I once hired a student because she told the story of her swim team experiences in college. Up at four in the morning and into the pool;

three hours of training, then a day in class. It told me everything I needed to know about her work ethic. She *showed* me by example. She didn't *tell* me.

> *Show, don't tell.*

Act enthusiastic

My advice appears to be inconsistent. On the one hand, I'm suggesting that you need to know yourself and project your values. On the other, I'm telling you that if you simply behave as your ordinary, relaxed self, you have no chance of getting hired. Confusing, isn't it?

A little acting is part of the job of a successful professional. You have to put on a game face for judges when you're in court or for the opposite side in a negotiation; when you lose a motion and have to convey to the client your ongoing optimism about the prospects of your case; when you lose at trial but convince the client you can win on appeal; when you wake up depressed and need to project enthusiasm at a client prospect lunch. Eventually you'll discover that, as a leader, rather than giving in to doubt, you need to project confidence and optimism. In short, acting is a prerequisite for professionals!

The person you need to project in an interview is the best version of "you." The one who people want to have on their team. The one who has a fascinating story to tell and can do so in a way that allows me, the interviewer, to feel your emotion. I need to experience your passion. I will give you some strategies to showcase yourself in the next chapter.

Controlling the agenda

The worst thing that can happen to you in an interview or any meeting is losing control of your agenda. You are there to sell, but so often the interviewers take over, leaving you little time to project yourself.

Of all my articling interviews I remember only one vividly: my forty minutes at Davies Ward & Beck[10]—a Toronto-based firm I desperately wanted to work at. The interviewer spent the better part of the interview selling *me* on *them*. I learned his brother played in the NHL. I left that meeting with him knowing nothing of my family. I doubt I spoke for even two minutes in total. I sat there wondering to myself, "When is it my turn?" The short answer was never. Did I leave with a chip on my shoulder? I'm still thinking about it over forty years later.

My wife, Sharon, attended ten interviews with major accounting firms and received ten offers. She walked into each interview having researched the firm and its strengths and weaknesses, according to what was available in the public domain and from senior acquaintances who had worked in the firm. Sharon did her homework thoroughly, prepared her questions, then interviewed the interviewers. They were enthralled, to the point that years later even the firms that did not hire her still remember her. I can assure you that the major law firms who rejected me as a student have no recollection of me. I allowed myself to be forgettable. It didn't *happen* to me—I *allowed* it to happen to me.

One final piece of advice, from the other side of the desk. I have interviewed countless candidates and had to choose between them to build an organization. I saw these interviews as my opportunity both to market the virtues of the culture of my organization, and to convince the candidates that my organization was a place that would embrace them. I needed them to feel that I needed them and that choosing my firm would be the best decision of their lives.

In short, I wanted them to leave the process wanting me. I wanted to hire people who honestly wanted to work at my firm. I wanted candidates to consider my firm something special, even if it wasn't for them. That was part of my sales job!

10. Now Davies Ward Phillips & Vineberg LLP.

For me to hire someone, it was not enough that they were excellent. They needed to project just how fortunate they were to have the opportunity to join us. I had to perceive that my firm was their first choice. Perality at work. I wanted my firm to be the place where everyone wanted to work, so we could select only those who fit best.

Your goal as the job candidate should be to leave every interviewer with the impression that their firm is a place you would sell your soul to work at. That they are your first choice. When you have the luxury of choosing between offers, you can deal with that "problem."

Choosing the best place for you to work is the subject of the next chapter.

CHAPTER 4

The Fit That's Right for You

One of the first challenges in your career will be to determine where you are best suited to work. First is the question of venue: large firm, small firm, in-house, your own shop, government, non-profit, politics, business. Then comes the decision of your area(s) of practice. For lawyers: litigation, corporate, employment, family, criminal, just to name a few. For accountants: audit, tax, consulting, small business, large business, cost accounting. Perhaps you want to leave the profession entirely—maybe to join a business or start one yourself, to run a professional sports league, to become a political candidate, even to run the country. The choices are virtually limitless.

The best advice those of us with more experience can give you is to keep an open mind.

Finding your fit

There are a number of misconceptions about finding a job. The first is that you need to figure out who the company is looking for and then tailor yourself to fit their mould.

I mentioned Jim Beqaj's book, *True Fit*, in the previous chapter. According to Jim, every workplace has its own ethos or internal environment, philosophy, and approach that either fits your personality or doesn't. You should not be surprised that the closer you are naturally aligned to the ethos of your workplace, the more likely it is that you will succeed and thrive there. The converse is also true. If you work for a place where you have nothing in common with the others, you will discover, all too soon, that it's a lonely place to work—like high school without friends all over again.

If you walk into an interview expecting you need to "play the part" of the candidate they are looking for, you might get the job and wish you hadn't.

Erin O'Toole is the leader of the Conservative Party of Canada. I recently interviewed him about key moments in his legal career. He began as a student and young associate at one of the country's leading firms, then headed in-house for a number of years before heading back to private practice at another national firm, where he launched his political career.

"I was born with public service in my blood," Erin tells me. "When I started practice, I mistakenly believed that the top-rated firms would want me to follow that passion as part of my early development. I wanted to get out and meet people, develop my own practice, and spend time investing in my need to serve, as I had when I joined Canada's armed forces."

The firm had other plans for Erin. Their philosophy was that their job was to teach their young associates the practice of law. Nothing but the law. No practice development. No "extra-curriculars," as Erin calls it. There was too much work to go around, which may have suited some of the new hires—but not Erin. After he spent a few years learning lessons from some fantastic mentors in the litigation group, Erin moved in-house.

"A little ironic that to get through the interview process at the top firms, you need a long list of extra-curriculars, but once you get inside, they want you to abandon them."

Erin's comments are a common refrain from a number of associates I've spoken to, who "lived the dream" of articling at a big-name firm.

One promising young woman, Aden, has the classic outgoing personality: charming, gregarious, and smart, the kind of person who would make an incredible transactional lawyer. When she completed law school, she landed at one of the country's most influential firms. Here is how Aden explained her experience:

"From an early stage of my development, I felt the need to share my views, to go after new clients, to talk to the firm's clients. I needed to do more than just push paper, yet that's not what the firm wanted.

"They had more than enough clients. They expected my cohort of young associates to put our heads down, sit in our offices, and just do the work. After a couple of years, I began to hate the experience, except the odd time the partners needed someone to go out and hold a client's hand in a tense situation. They knew I had that talent, but I was just like a role player coming off the bench." Aden felt like she was wasting the potential she had to be an entrepreneur. It was in her blood.

"Why are all big firms like that?" she asked.

"They're not all alike," I said. "You would have been a perfect fit for my firm, where we valued lawyers with an entrepreneurial spirit. You simply chose the wrong firm for you!"

Do your homework

These days it's easy to collect info on firms and their professionals online.[11] Remember, though, that while all the big firms may look the same in size and scope, each has a distinct personality and set of internal values.

Erin O'Toole put it very well to me. "The top dozen firms all have excellent lawyers and impressive clients. Don't be swayed by the firm rankings established by the professional magazines. It'll be years until that matters."

Decide first what matters to you. If you have an interest in working pro bono, participating in politics, engaging early in your career with firm clients, or developing your own clients, use the interview to see if that syncs with what the firm expects. The interview is your chance to test how the interviewers behave. Pay attention to how their answers to your questions match with what their promotional material says they value and with what you're looking for in a firm.

---

11. Keep in mind that websites and biographies are meant to be promotional. They reveal certain facts, but not character.

What questions should you ask?

When you research legal firm websites, they all look like they've been developed by the same marketing company. Here are a few modern-day bromides that show up everywhere: "We value diversity," or "We offer innovative solutions to clients." Everyone says it, but who actually lives it?

If, for example, diversity is an issue that you care about, how can you distinguish among firms? This is where your observation and interview skills should come in handy.

Pay attention to the following:

- Who attends the interviews?

- Who are the key people running the programs?

- Are they diverse?

- What challenges has the firm faced along the road to achieving diversity?

Like a good detective, dig beyond what is on the website. Speak to associates who typify diversity at the firm. Are they welcoming, or are they warning you away?

What about innovation? Is it limited to allowing professionals to work from home? You might ask the following questions:

- How do you train for innovation in your young professionals?

- Do you involve students and young professionals in the development of your new technology?

- How is the firm's budget being spent on innovation?

These are all questions most interviewees would not think to ask. Those candidates are so focused on themselves that they're not focused on the place they are choosing.

Every firm has a website, but if technology turns your crank, you might want a firm at the cutting edge of practising with newly developed technology. You may want to ask questions such as these:

- Do you have any areas of service that are married to new technology?

- Do you consider yourself a leader or follower of tech trends?

The answers will be revealing.

Most firms are very conservative and slow to move. Few, if any, want to be the trendsetter. They will make radical change only when a black swan, like COVID-19, comes along. If you're looking for a trend-setting environment, then the "big-firm experience" is probably not for you. Firms tend to run the way they run, regardless of inefficiencies or quirks, because that is what makes the people within them comfortable.

Another question for a firm is:

- What is your sixty-second infomercial?

You might want to save that one for a second round, or the "drinks and dinner" interview, when you can pose it to a number of different people over the course of an evening. In high-functioning organizations, every employee knows what their firm is all about and will give you a crisp and consistent answer, more or less the same regardless of whom you ask. Average firms usually don't even know where to begin answering the question.

"Here is the client base we represent. Here is how we market ourselves. When we say we are this kind of firm, here are some examples of what we do every day to drive that home." This is the beginning of a sixty-second answer that suggests the firm knows who they are and what their employees have in common. It will also tell you immediately whether you will fit. Are those the kind of values that speak to you?

> *If you are personally aligned with the firm's values, you are far more likely to enjoy going to work every day.*

If you don't feel a rapport with the interviewers or other employees, it's usually a sign that the firm is not going to be a fit for you. Our biases tend to have us like people who share our values and interests.

The final warning in this chapter is to be careful what you wish for. I've interviewed countless young associates who matched with the firm of their choice and ended up hating every moment, putting in the time, like convicts in prison, until they had accumulated enough experience to pad their résumés for the next stop. Many of them never return to private practice.

We will take a more in-depth look into what qualities in-house counsel are looking for in Chapter 15.

What about compensation?

This is perhaps the most difficult question to answer in this book, since so much about compensation is tied to your stage and bargaining position. As a general principle, the less experience you have, the less negotiating power you have.

A critical issue in negotiation is the amount of leverage you have. For example, years ago American firms actively recruited the best Canadian law students, so the larger Canadian firms had to raise the level of student salaries to make sure they stayed. Even in those circumstances, students took what was offered.

As you progress, your negotiating position may improve. Do you have any clients of your own? What are they worth to the prospective firm? Have you developed a sought-after expertise? Are you at a level of practice where there is major demand? The more experienced you are, the more complicated the answer. More on that in my next book.

When you can't find your fit

All very well and good, but what happens when you're out of work, need a job, and you don't get your fit-pick? The age-old question: when to abandon your ideals and take the job you know doesn't suit you in order to pad your résumé with experience. This is particularly the case in tough economic markets. Is it better to be looking or to be working?

Wayne Levin, retired general counsel and chief strategic officer at LA film studio Lionsgate, provides this advice in countless mentoring sessions:

"I suggest to recent graduates to look for a job for three to six months and then take anything, because looking for a job while you have a job and are eating is better than the alternative. You have to get your feet wet even if you don't like the pool.

"For the really qualified, I tell them to stomach a big firm environment, if they can find one, for at least two years because they need to learn their craft. Fit at that point in their careers, in my opinion, is not a huge criterion. Fit and interests can come later.

"They may hate the experience but in terms of their overall career, they should treat it as an investment."

As long as you understand that the choice is yours, and the investments and sacrifices, also yours.

CHAPTER 5

Impress with Your Communication

The following three chapters deal with the single most important art for all professionals and particularly for lawyers. Communication, whether oral, written, or conveyed by non-verbal cues, is essential to your success. Regardless of how smart or well prepared you may be, if you can't convey your point in a clear, concise, and confident manner, you have lost.

The three Cs: confidence, clarity, crispness

Some of you may be naturals—extroverted by nature, the life of every party, confident on your feet, quick with a quip, naturally projecting an outward confidence. You were born to own a microphone.

Most of us are not. We never debated, because we found the very idea intimidating. We avoided situations requiring us to step up in front of a group. We were never the school keeners. I included myself in that lot of introverts, far more comfortable listening than speaking, rarely the person to ask the sage question that has every head in the classroom turning, or to venture a response to a Socratic question. I tend to think things through before I open my mouth.

If you're not a natural born extrovert, can you compete?

The good news is that the notion of the "born speaker" is the exception in life, rather than the rule. Barack Obama rode his speaking ability to the White House. He has the gift. The rest of us have to work at it.

As with any other skill, some may have more natural ability than others. But with practice and direction, you can learn, and with patience and determination, excel, at speaking.

If you're interested in a podcast break, you might appreciate this five-step formula for feeling and appearing more confident:
Talkabouttalk.com/24-abcdes-of-communication-with-dr-andrea-wojnicki

I am living proof that determination and study can turn you into a more dynamic, effective, and comfortable speaker. I did not start out this way.

Let's begin with the negative role models in my life. So many lecturers drone on and on, pretending to be oblivious to the fact that most of their audience—at least me—has tuned them out. I'm lulled into a state where I'm not listening, until the inevitable happens—my eyes droop, then shut. Nothing has changed in forty years of listening to lifeless speakers.

In 1986 I inherited my first lecture course in business law at McGill University. My boss, the lecturer, was quite ill and I literally took the course over mid-semester, with no notice. I would scramble to prepare each lecture the night before, and one week I was working on a transaction and only had an hour to prepare. I was lecturing around two hundred students in a Roman-style amphitheatre. The people in the front row were level with me, but those in the rear had to be thirty feet up. Talk about an intimidating setup. Some of the material was particularly dry, such as teaching the four elements that make up a contract. However, I learned from an unexpected source how to get their attention.

Epiphany manifests from the most unusual sources. One Sunday morning I was flipping through the television stations and stopped in on a preacher. Normally these were the type of stations I channel-surfed. This time I tuned in for a few minutes; that was one of the best decisions of my life.

Talk about drama! The reverend begins in a low overtone, speaking slowly, telling a story about Jesus. As the story heads toward its moment of challenge, the preacher's voice picks up. He raises his pitch, his pace a little faster, his voice louder still as he rises to the pinnacle moment of the story. The moment of truth. The moment of personal challenge. Then he stops speaking.

The camera pans to the audience. They are enthralled. No one is looking at their watches. Every face is mesmerized. The speaker is in complete control. The hall is deathly quiet.

I count at least five seconds of silence. If you don't think that's a long time, then the next time you're speaking to someone, try the experiment. Stop speaking and count slowly to five in your head. It feels like forever.

After this eternity, he resumes speaking, now in a lower tone, as he explains the message of the story. Once more as he reaches the moral of the story he wants to emphasize, his voice becomes more excited, and when he finishes with the main point, he stops speaking.

What was it I learned that day and continue learning from these speakers? I didn't understand it at the time. I simply began to emulate the style, with outstanding audience response. My students were not sleeping. They laughed, they jumped into the conversation, they were excited, occasionally uncomfortable, but never bored and never, ever sleeping.

Keeping your audience's attention

John Miers, a professional speaking coach, who established the international speaking firm Black Isle Global, helped me to put it all in perspective many years ago. John explained that the average attention span was seven minutes. It is now dramatically shorter.[12]

12. A 2015 study conducted by Microsoft concluded that digital attention spans had shrunk to 8.25 seconds, slightly shorter than that of a goldfish.
https://time.com/3858309/attention-spans-goldfish/
Other marketing research suggests the average video attention span in 2015 was under three minutes.

That means that if you have to make a twenty-minute presentation, every few minutes you will lose your audience. They will drift. You need to change it up. Speed up; slow down; pause. Get excited, then bring the audience back down. Stop after you've made an important point—let it marinate.

At first blush, a speech appears to be a monologue. That is only true of a poor speaker.

> *When you speak, you are in a conversation—*
> *a dialogue with your audience.*

One of the most effective screenwriting teachers, Robert McKee, has explained that what may appear to be monologue, on the screen or in live theatre, is really dialogue with the audience. You need to tap into their stories, their emotions, and their lives to connect your story to theirs. This means you need to pause when you've made a point. Let the audience mentally connect the dots—between their experience and your words.

Most important, you need to keep the audience engaged in the conversation. How many times does a really good speaker have you thinking to yourself? I'm not speaking about the Socratic method of making your audience uncomfortable by asking them questions to lead them to your answer. I mean something more subtle, more powerful.

The impact of storytelling

When you lecture or present, you are storytelling. People do not connect with facts or argument. They connect with stories. If you are presenting only facts and evidence without context, your presentation is boring. By adding story, the factual presentation has context.

I spent twenty-five years making speeches at my law firm, and if you were to conduct a survey, there is only one that people still speak about today. They call it the Blueberry Speech.

As an experiment I had decided to open my annual holiday party speech to the staff with a recollection of how my favourite childhood memory was picking wild blueberries with my grandfather. I paused at the end of the story to let it sink in, hoping each staff member would connect to some warm childhood memory of their own. I went on to speak for another ten minutes about the firm and how we were all connected to one another in ways we could not comprehend.

Not a soul could tell you what else I spoke about that night or in the countless speeches that came before or after. However, they will remember vividly the tables they were sitting at when I spoke about the blueberries and how it made them feel.

Emotional connection, pacing, varying tonality, storytelling: all these are at least as important as the content of your speech. Your audience will not remember the facts, but they will always remember how you made them feel—their emotional connection to your story. The speakers we remember share that skill.

More on storytelling in the following podcast:
Talkabouttalk.com/42-telling-your-story-with-norman-bacal

Write it down

Over the years I have become more comfortable speaking with a set of notes in outline form. They're very helpful when I lose my train of thought or can't remember where to go next. I never try to memorize a speech. My brain does not work that way.

Ask me to memorize facts and repeat them, and I'll get hopelessly lost. And I still get nervous if asked to introduce a speaker—too many biographical details to remember. The same goes with any presentation on technical material. I write things down: the numbers and names and facts, and I refer to them as needed.

Some people need to write out more than just an outline or a set of facts. It's not a sin to write out your material and read it. But it *is* a sin to have your head down while you do it. Do that and you lose your audience.

Here is one trick to help you present effectively: start by printing out your talk in very large font on two-thirds of a page.

About this size,

with no more than a phrase on a line,

so you can pick up your phrases in chunks

and continually look up.

The equivalent of a teleprompter.

Try not to speak while you are reading.

Gulp the words. Then look up.

Speak while you survey the audience.

Take a break.

Look down and gulp more phrases.

Look up and continue speaking.

More useful tips

1. Eye contact with the audience is critical. Focus on three or four people in the room in different locations. Those are the people you need to make eye contact with, to see if you are connecting. Those are the people you are having the conversation with. You can see the look in their eyes. Your sample audience. Are they nodding their heads? Are they responding to your eyes? When you raise your voice, do they look excited? Are their eyes drifting? If so, it's time to shock them with a silence or a change in your voice modulation—a wake-up call.

2. Practise your first sixty seconds until you know it cold. Record it half a dozen times on your smartphone and play it back. You will see an improvement. The first minute is when your nerves are not yet relaxed, when you tend to speak too quickly because the adrenaline is pushing you. That's the time you need to get settled. Slow yourself down.

    Very often I'll take a walk before a speech and practise my opening twenty times. Trying to memorize never works for me. Some people have talent for memorizing lines, but I was always terrible. The more I try to get it perfect the more I fumble. Instead I will repeat the first sixty seconds without notes, knowing that each time I am telling the story a little differently. That's perfectly okay.

    I'm not going to sugarcoat it. The very notion of having to get through that first minute sends so many of us into a panic attack. That's your fear speaking to you—trying to control you. We'll spend an entire chapter on fear and how to turn it to your advantage further on. For now, practise with audiences, whether friends, the mirror, or your smartphone, as you slowly build confidence.

    It isn't about positive messaging in the mirror. It's about creating a small success before you go public, then building on that success in tiny increments. You may never completely get over the fear, but you do have to park it somewhere so that it cannot hurt you.

3. You need to experiment and find the style best suited to you. Maybe it's your dry humour, your inbred cynicism, or your own life story of overcoming some adversity that can connect you to the audience.

4. Give your speech the way you would tell a story. When you tell a story, you don't think about getting each word right. You think about narrating the story. And if you're anything like many of my friends, every time you tell it, the details will change a little or be emphasized differently. That's the way you want to communicate when you give a speech.

5. Focus on pace. Take breaks and count them out in your head. Three seconds of silence is much longer than you can imagine. It can be a powerful way to get your audience thinking about what you just said. You want them to be conversing with you in their heads, and the only way they can do that is if you give them time to respond.

Use PowerPoint effectively or not at all

I must confess to a bias. I rarely use electronic assistance when I speak. Though it does have a time and a place, PowerPoint (or similar apps) is often a crutch that hobbles a speaker more than it helps them.

John Miers taught me that the human brain has difficulty reading and listening simultaneously. You can do one or the other at a time efficiently. When combined, you do neither well. Those who claim to be efficient multitaskers are lying to themselves about this particular ability. Has anyone ever walked in on you and said something while you were reading or concentrating? How many times have you asked them to please repeat? Either your audience is listening, or they're reading. Probably they are not being efficient at either, if you keep interrupting one with the other.

The worst transgression of all is putting up a slide that summarizes what you're saying; that's treating your audience like bird brains. Why do you need to repeat out loud what they're reading on the screen? We've all seen terrible speakers (some of them very successful people) do just that. Too many words on a slide, or a font that is too small, means the audience can't read it at all. Why not just beg them to dislike you?

It's an especially poor idea to put up a slide while you're making the point. Your audience will not know whether to listen or read. Instead, use PowerPoint to reinforce your point. Maybe it's a graph that illustrates a point you just made. Or a cartoon to make the audience laugh. Put the slide up *after* you've made your point to drive the point home. If you have a graph, explain what you want the audience to look at.

There will be times where you're asked by the people who organize the presentation to prepare a hard copy of your slides. I find the hard copy presentation a distraction. I am that guy who gets bored while the speaker is taking me through the introductory material on page 5, when all I care about is finding the info I want on page 22. Except I don't know it's on page 22 until I find it myself. I am neither listening nor reading. I'm shuffling and frustrated. You've already lost.

Instead, I suggest handing out the hard copy of the slides after you're finished, and only then. Use it as an audience takeaway to reinforce your key messages.

If you're making a presentation to people who *require* a slide book, like investment bankers, then when you focus the audience on a page, *stop talking*. Give them time to read it. Don't repeat the message. Reinforce the key messages once they look up from the page.

The same goes for a presentation to a judge. If you want her to read a handout or a quote, let her read it quietly. Stop talking. Shut up. Otherwise you're working against yourself. If there is a line you want the judge to focus on, wait until she raises her head and makes eye contact. Then direct her to the point.

Once she's done reading, pick the key excerpt you want to read aloud and add the emphasis. Federal Court of Appeal Justice Stratas taught his mentees to follow up using this opening: ***"I just want to highlight one key element (or sentence)…"***

While this chapter focused on the art of public speaking, the next chapter will deal with a more subtle art form—but one that may be even more critical: the art of listening.

CHAPTER 6

Communication Is a Two-way Street

What is communication, if not a two-way street? That's the theory, but in practice it's much more complicated. You might believe that the key skill as a professional (and in particular in lawyering) is effectively making your point. That is less than half correct. Before you can convince anyone of the strength of your argument, a single skill, possibly your weakest, must be sharpened.

"Courage is what it takes to stand up and speak; courage is also what it takes to sit down and listen."
— WINSTON CHURCHILL

By far, the toughest communication skill for lawyers is listening. We are trained to be compelling with our arguments. We are under the somewhat incorrect impression that to be compelling and convincing we must focus primarily on what we have to say and how we say it. However, we increase our credibility when we demonstrate an ability to hear the other side.

Lawyers may spend hours preparing arguments for the court room, a mediation, a presentation, or a negotiation. However, if we do not master the art of listening, we run the risk that our arguments are not being heard. I know that sounds contradictory. What does my inability to listen have to do with your inability to hear what I'm telling you?

Can you listen while you're speaking?

Let's begin with the way others behave when you're speaking. It's a general misconception that we listen with our ears; this is only partly true. According to Dr. Andrea Wojnicki, so much of communication is non-verbal and implicit. Tone of voice, facial expression, and body language, among other things, can tell you so much about the impact that your ideas are having on another. Our eyes are critical listening tools.

When we're trying to emphasize a position, are the listeners nodding their heads in approval or shaking them? Are their facial features tight? Are they making eye contact, avoiding contact, or looking off in disgust? Are they smiling or frowning? Do they have blank looks, suggesting they're bored, disinterested, or not understanding? All these reactions allow you to decode whether and to what extent you are connecting.

Effective listeners take note of these reactions and adjust. If I sense hostility, I can surmise that my ideas are being rejected. Perhaps I need to take a step back and deal with the root of the hostility before the other party is ready to listen to the message.

I faced this on countless occasions as managing partner, trying to convince reluctant lawyers to accept a message I had to deliver. My eyes could perceive that what I said was being met with hostility, or worse, with an indifferent look or response. In other situations, I was expecting debate or disagreement and was met with stony silence. It is true that sometimes silence speaks louder than words. In those situations, I had to step backward, understanding there might be issues impacting the person I was speaking to that had to be dealt with first. Until I listened to their concerns and acknowledged them, they were not prepared to listen to me.

Conversing by phone deprives you of many non-verbal cues you might catch with your other senses. By far the worst way to conduct an argument is through text (email, text message, or written correspondence), where tone is near impossible to read. Humour and irony in a text response are often confused with anger, and the dreaded CAPS leave all kinds of room for misinterpretation. Email and text messages are fantastic media for exchanging factual communication. However, they leave far too much room for misunderstanding in emotional exchanges.

For more on listening, listen in here:
Talkabouttalk.com/41-listening-with-norman-bacal

Listening in an argument

As I mentioned previously, despite the general popularity of the concept of multitasking, the brain has difficulty doing two things at once.[13] Listening while you are busy thinking is exactly the sort of situation where things break down. The same goes for the party you are engaged with.

My first boss was a tax litigator. Jean Potvin had a unique ability to absorb arguments I had spent tens of hours preparing, then masterfully present them in court as if he had done all the work himself. On some occasions we spent hours arguing through the preparation, with him failing to understand what I was telling him. The lightbulb finally went off for me when I figured out that in order to convince Jean, I had to have him repeat my argument in his words. Until he did that, he could not understand me. That was his way of listening.

Like most people, when I get upset or disagree, I begin to interrupt and stop listening. What I have to say is more important than what you have to say. Some kind of override upsets my rational

---

13. In a speech at West Point in October 2009, author William Deresiewicz quotes a Stanford study on whether the skills to multitask developed by the current generation of college students exceed those of previous generations. His conclusion: "…The answer…is that they don't. The enhanced cognitive abilities the researchers expected to find…the mental faculties that enable people to multitask effectively, were simply not there…the more people multitask, the worse they are, not just at other mental abilities, but at multitasking itself."
https://theamericanscholar.org/solitude-and-leadership/#.X3KCRe17k2x

brain, which would normally tell me to let the other person finish. It is a battle I sometimes lose. ***When I stop listening, I am working against myself. I know it, but I can't help it.***

So how do we learn to control ourselves in those moments? There is no simple answer, unless we set ourselves up for success before we start. Here are two examples of incredibly effective techniques.

David Roebuck, in his lifetime one of the finest litigators I've had the privilege to work with, used a technique that he passed along to his mentees. They call it "the pause," not much different than the pause we discussed that can be used in a lecture. It's very powerful to come to a full stop after making an effective point in an argument, so that the other party can absorb that point. Rushing from one good point to another through the use of "and furthermore…" has you working against yourself. They can't hear you while you continue talking after your last point. Let it sink in. Test the reaction.

The best listener I ever met employed a unique listening method that was so awesome it is worth sharing. When Frances expected an argument, she would sit down opposite the person in conflict and let them speak. While they were speaking, she took copious notes. For any of you who have debated, this is the exact same process as when your opponent has the floor. One by one she would list the critical points and jot brief notes, perhaps a reminder of a key critical rebuttal. When the opponent stopped speaking, only then would Frances ask, "Are you finished?"

Once she had that confirmation, she would respond to the arguments point by point. Sound simple? Almost no one does it. In case you're wondering, invariably when Frances begins her rebuttal, the other party will get excited and interrupt. Her stock response is to stop and state, "When you were speaking, I listened quietly. I am asking you to show me the same courtesy." The one thing Frances never does is shout over an interruption. She stops, and rather than engaging in argument, she points out her opponents' inability to control themselves and waits until they are ready to listen. After all, what is the point of arguing with someone who is no longer listening to you?[14]

Frances is sought after all over the world for her business negotiation skills, and her ability to manage very difficult conflict situations. This may be one reason why.

Regardless of whether Frances and her opponent can come to agreement, the process eliminates the excitement and bad feelings generated by the discourtesy of interruption. After all, when you interrupt you are basically signalling to the other party that what you have to say is more important. You are working against yourself.

The value of appearing patient

Justice Lori Anne Thomas of the Ontario Court of Justice, until recently a criminal defence lawyer in Toronto and the president of the Canadian Association of Black Lawyers , tells me that she is not a patient person by nature. "*Appearing* patient, however, is a useful quality in convincing a court of the merit of your case. In one particular situation I was certain that a matter could be dealt with in under ten minutes if only the judge had been prepared to give me the floor. Instead it took the judge hours to address my case. All I wanted to do was interrupt and take over. Instead I waited. It earned me great favour with the judge." Patience and listening: an awesome combination.

14. My litigator friend tells me this is a very useful technique in court. When the other lawyer interrupts, my friend sits down and stops speaking. It unnerves the other lawyer and gets the judge really irritated at the interrupter. Does that help the case? After all, judges are human.

CHAPTER 7

Writing Skills

I may not have interviewed well, but by the time I graduated law school, I could churn out a very competent factum and memos the likes of which would have turned the head of Supreme Court justices. It took me a few years in practice to work out that my lengthy treatises were of no interest to clients. Like the eight-pager on a title search, where a driveway might have been subject to a fifty-year-old right of way, the legal issues were fascinating. But not to a client.

No client is reading an eight-page memo about a driveway. No business client is reading an eight-page memo about anything. They're probably not willing to pay for it either. Clients don't want erudite. The Supreme Court wants erudite. The rest of us want easy-to-read answers. Through my development and after many hits and misses, I figured out what senior lawyers who asked me to do work and what clients want. So keep reading.

Memos

Whether you're writing for a more senior lawyer or directly for a client, you must apply the same high level of rigour to your research as you did in law school. But presentation skills in the real world of short attention spans, and the quest to solve problems quickly and proficiently, are dramatically different from what you learned at school.

Law school hammers home the notion that few questions have black-and-white answers. The same is true in accounting. The professional world of theory is filled with doubt. Law students are trained to analyze those doubts and consider all the dissenting judgments that might one day become the law to get an A+ grade. If you want to become a CPA, in order to pass the final exams for certification, you're training to hit a marking key of points. The way the books you study to pass professional-school qualification exams train you for a specific purpose having nothing to do with your career.

In practice there are shades, likelihoods of outcomes. What's more, while addressing those shades and the risks associated with a course of action, you can easily become the client's worst enemy, paralyzed by doubt. Clients care only about the solution, not the shades or the theory, and that is where so many practitioners find themselves at cross purposes with their clients. They become so eager to point out all the pitfalls they've been trained to look for, the risks they're hired to analyze, that their writing focuses on the risks and fails to highlight the solution.

The most common wedge that drives clients away from their legal advisors resides in a complaint that I've heard voiced thousands of times: *"I'm tired of being advised what I can't do. All I want is some practical advice as to what I should do."*

Our problem in the legal profession is that we like to analyze risk, but we don't like to take it. For so many of us, that is the reason we became lawyers. "Leave the risk to the business people," one senior lawyer suggested to me many years ago. The clients understand that you are not there to assume the risk. You are there to help mitigate the risk by suggesting a best course of action. Sometimes that best course leaves the client open to some risk. Your job is to help them decide. You recommend, but the client decides!

Even worse than that common complaint, above, is what I would label "thorough memorandum syndrome." In my early years I may have done an exceedingly good job pointing out all the risks and making all the arguments and counter-arguments. And some lawyers insist the client ought to read everything, process the information, and make a decision. That is the road to nowhere.

> *Clients do not like and rarely read rambling memos.*

They don't have the time, energy, or bandwidth to get through them. They are facing real-world problems, not hypothetical law school dilemmas. Instead they complain, "I have no idea what you're advising me to do."[15]

Early in my career, one senior tax lawyer was well known for his ninety-page opinions. They satisfied his intellectual curiosity and his hubris—but I doubt they did much for his clients.

Clients want to be led. They want an answer. They want an analysis of the risk associated with the decision. Sometimes there are two options. They want to know on balance which is better, particularly when the differences are marginal.

How do we deal with these challenges?

"Begin at the beginning and go on till you come to the end: then stop." It worked for Lewis Carroll and other novelists. Not as well for lawyers.

> *I recommend that your memos start with the end.*

Create no more than a one-page executive summary. (Most clients will not read page 2.) The first paragraph outlines the question, to make certain you've got that right. The second summarizes the solution, along with a brief estimation of the risks associated with the course of action. The rest of your work stays in your file. You need to have done the work, but few people care to read the subtle reasoning or the trail of arguments and counter-arguments leading to the conclusion.

---

15. No rule is universal. There are situations where standard-form lengthy memos are generated by major law firms to deal with issues on common large transactions they undertake. I often wonder if they are meant to be read, rather than stuffed in a drawer by the general counsel of the client. The utility of the memo is to outline the checklist of events, the rationale behind them, and the duties and obligations of the teams of lawyers on the file.

Developing the discipline to answer a question and recommend a course of action in one crisp page of prose is the most challenging task for a young lawyer. Some senior lawyers are still working on it!

The course of a war, and perhaps American history, turned on 272 words, uttered on a bloodied battlefield. The Gettysburg Address speaks for itself.

Save the lengthy analysis for an appendix or part two of the memo that you stick in the file so you can prove you've covered all the issues. Your insurer will be happy. So will your client.[16]

Before we leave the subject of memos, there is one general point about all written communication that must be reinforced. Make sure that the grammar, spelling, and punctuation in your work has been double- and triple-checked. Nothing speaks of sloppiness more than these types of errors. Joseph Groia, a prominent Ontario litigator, tells all his associates to "proofread to perfection."

Speed of response time

When I began practice, fax machines had not yet been invented. The closest thing to instantaneous written advice was the telex. I can only recall one client in California that insisted on it. Most written correspondence was mailed. One particular client admonished me for sending documents related to his late mother's estate by courier. He thought the cost was profligate spending of his inheritance.

Today the instantaneous response has become what's expected, keeping pace with the instantaneous movement of world economies. Here are points to consider:

---

16. For every rule there are exceptions that I have experienced. Sophisticated in-house counsel will be very interested in that appendix, for example, when dealing with a subject that the client wants and needs to be educated about (for example, the legal and political landscape affecting a particular domestic industry that a foreign client is considering expanding into, or a brief that rationalizes why you see merit in filing leave to appeal to the Supreme Court on an important case that the client lost on appeal).

Texts and emails

Texts and emails are the bane of our existence these days. By tapping on their mobile devices, clients can reach us and seek our advice twenty-four seven. If we don't respond quickly enough, are we providing the best service?

Given the speed with which we are expected to reply, texts and emails are open to many pitfalls. Here are a few:

1. **The typo:** Nothing says shoddy work more than a lawyer who gives advice replete with typos, or shorthand spelling, or the dreaded meme, gif, or emoji. Nothing shouts unprofessionalism more than that yellow smiley face with sunglasses.

2. **Misinterpretation:** There is little room in emails and texts to express tone. Humour can easily be mistaken for sarcasm, and CAPS for anger or outrage rather than emphasis. Try to restrict your emails and texts to conveying information rather than emotion.

3. **The answer on the fly:** I have to confess I am sometimes so anxious to respond to clients that when I hear the *ping* while in a client meeting or stopped at a red light, I can't help myself and reply in haste. (When in the car, I pull over first. That does not excuse my stupidity.) It took me years to break the addiction. Occasionally my split-second response reflects a poor understanding of a quickly dashed-off client question. In my case these days, it usually involves getting an errand wrong.

   Most questions posed by clients require some quiet reflection. Taking time to think has become a lost art. The client may not have framed the question well, or they may not have considered critical facts as pertinent. More investigation may be necessary before answering. Sometimes you just have to let the problem "marinate," or as my mentor used to say, "I need to cogitate," though that one always sounded better when translated into French.

   So how do we handle the enormous pressure created when clients expect a quick response?

The answer lies in early acknowledgment, communication, and setting expectations promptly. If you're in a meeting with a client, you do not want to be working on another client's problems. If you don't have the luxury of an assistant to monitor your messages and respond, then go with a virtual alternative: an automatic response explaining when you will be able to reply will usually do the trick. If you've sent out one of those, then make sure you follow up.

Keep your promises in order to keep Perality's two heads, perception and reality, aligned. If the situation is urgent, then you have to triage. Decide whether you need to take a short break from a meeting or call to handle an emergency. As in an emergency room, triage has to come before the care or the cure. This doesn't only apply to lawyers in private practice. Triage is a critical skill for effective in-house counsel advising the business unit.

> *Instantaneous written communication has reset client service expectations.*

Controlling expectations

The problem with texts and emails is that clients can *always* reach us on our smartphones. How do you deal with the client who has an idea and sends a quick email, assuming you're holding your phone ready to respond immediately, whether at two in the morning or on Sunday afternoon when you're out with the family? How and when do you respond? Do you respond at all?

The approach I recommend is consistent with improving client service. Set expectations and meet them. Be clear in your communications and be consistent. Within those parameters there are as many alternatives as there are client types.

Set boundaries on your availability. Back when I practised karate, I set aside two hours every Monday and Wednesday lunchtime and let clients know, as I onboarded them, that I was not reachable or available for meetings in those time slots. I treated karate as an important business meeting.[17]

If you spend weekends or certain hours of the evening with your family, tell your clients that you'll be available outside those hours.

If you want to triage for emergency requests from clients, then set up a protocol for how they let you know something requires immediate attention.

Most of the problems professionals face in setting boundaries with their clients emerge directly from their unwillingness to communicate. That kind of conversation makes many professionals uncomfortable. The likely cause is fear of rejection—one more fear to push through if you want some control in your personal life. (We'll discuss fear in Chapter 9.)

Get into the habit of ensuring that your clients have clear expectations, so you can meet those expectations. If you have a client who insists on regularly testing your boundaries, then you have a decision to make. But it's your decision. Frustration and anger emerge from powerlessness, from inequality of bargaining power. Remember, you set the limits, you set the expectations, and you decide how you want to live and how you want to work.

There are consequences associated with our life choices. You only fail when you fail to accept that fact.

For more on this subject the following podcast will help:
Talkabouttalk.com/37-phone-or-email

We'll focus in Chapter 11 on other ways of managing client expectations. Surprisingly, most clients are quite trainable.

---

17. That's how I made it to my *sandan*, or third degree black belt. That and fourteen years of dedicated practice.

CHAPTER 8

There's More to Solving Problems Than Meets the Eye

In university the mantra for exams is "do the required." Study a situation where the facts are known and the problems elaborated. You succeed by considering and analyzing the issues presented.

As a young associate, you advance one level. You step into the start or middle of a litigation, or you are given a piece of an evolving file to deal with. What lands on your desk has been filtered through the mind and process of someone more senior. The facts are presented, your role established, and your task defined.

But none of this prepares you for the moment when the file is yours from beginning to end. This happens more often than you might think in an in-house position. Daniel Lo, originally from Mississauga, Ontario, was recently hired by a major investment bank in Singapore. In his first month on the new job, Daniel was asked to make a legal decision in relation to a billion dollars of assets. "Just don't be wrong," he was told by the business unit.

That case is a bit extreme, but many small in-house departments require you to get up to speed on the business issues quickly. You need to understand the business before you can give any kind of worthwhile advice.

In a large firm you will be coddled a little more. You may be shielded for a number of years, and the transition to independence may be slow to arrive. But if you're on your own or in a small boutique, the day will rapidly come when you're responsible from the first call with the client, through the meetings, the strategy sessions, the decision on how to proceed, to the inevitable confrontation with another party, whether it's negotiating, concluding an agreement, or threatening or taking legal action.

Solving the problem may be easy or difficult. The challenge for us as lawyers (unless we're responding to a particular problem posed by an in-house legal department), is figuring out the precise nature of the problem. Unlike at law school, the true facts underpinning any legal problem are never given to you. Clients often take you on a walk through the woods, where it's so easy to lose sight of the forest for the trees. Sometimes they even obfuscate—it's no different from a doctor asking patients about their lifestyle and receiving an unrealistic picture because nobody wants to admit to eating two Big Macs after everybody goes to bed.

> *Before we can solve a problem, we need to frame it.*

Many clients (again, excluding the world of in-house legal departments) come to us with a problem, but they don't know the outcome they want. Or they know exactly what they want but they can't have it, because they don't have either the time, the money, or the leverage. Or they haven't considered the extraneous factors beyond their control that may have a bearing on the outcome, or the speed at which they need to solve the problem.

To do that we need to spend time understanding context, surrounding facts, and extraneous factors, which may not be obvious to the client. David Roebuck, whom I mentioned in Chapter 6, was a commercial litigator and a brilliant strategist. From him I learned that the key to helping clients is listening carefully, diagnosing the real problem, then helping clients strategize their way out of the mess they've gotten themselves into. Sage advice that David applied on a daily basis.

The root cause versus the symptoms

The matter begins with the client explaining their problem. Often the problem is presented through a lens that's focused on the wrong object. This is where listening intently and asking probing questions are essential. Your principal task is to focus the camera on the right object.

The client will provide you with their interpretation of the facts, but that interpretation will often be premised on a bias, a preconceived notion, or a solution the client has concocted. The client has not been trained in the law. Sometimes they get it right, but more often they're missing a key understanding that requires a reinterpretation of the facts.

Let's compare this situation to one you may be more familiar with: when you worry that you may be sick. While you're not trained in medicine, if you're experiencing symptoms, you might have paid a visit to Dr. Google to learn some of the possible diagnoses and to learn the medical lingo before seeing the doctor. When you finally get worried enough to see a doctor, you may have a sense of what the problem is and the language to explain it.

After listening to your concerns, your doctor will ask a series of questions, politely ignoring your diagnosis. Some of those questions will elicit responses about other symptoms you've been ignoring, or had not thought were relevant. The diagnosis may be something very different from what you suspected.

Life as a lawyer is no different. Like a thorough diagnostician, your job is to take the client back to the beginning of the story, sometimes before the beginning. This requires careful listening, understanding the right questions to ask, and accumulating background information that might be relevant to solving the problem.

Framing the problem

Discovering the facts is an important part of practice. Divining what is a critical fact and teasing that information out of the client is a skill that you develop by asking questions and listening. Taking cues from client reactions and asking more questions are essential to allow the framing of a problem, which is critical to being able to solve it.

Assisting your client in the framing is dependent on understanding everything possible about your client's situation. Just as a doctor would not try to diagnose you without taking a case history, you need to understand as much as you can about the client's overall situation if you want to make sure you understand the real problem, and not just treat the symptoms.

In order to frame your potential solutions, you then need to consider the following questions:

1. Are the client objectives achievable?

2. At what cost and on what time line?

3. Are there extraneous factors that will impact strategy?

4. What leverage does the client have?

5. What is the client's tolerance for risk and how do they define a successful outcome?

Understanding the client's goals and objectives

Providing effective service requires that you first determine what is important to the client, and then deliver on it. Unfortunately, it is so easy to get distracted by the details.

In my experience some of the biggest-name law firms teach their associates nothing about the art of distinguishing between the important and the trivial. They negotiate every point in an agreement with equal weight, wasting lots of time on matters of little consequence: whether a semicolon should be changed to a period; whether a boilerplate clause that your firm uses is better than the otherwise suitable clause of the other lawyer; whether the appropriate notice period should be ten days or three weeks.

Perhaps that's easier than focusing on the business issues driving the client that require particular attention. Most clients could not care less about perfect grammar, unless it interferes with a clear understanding of the business points. If you're trying to deliver value by the hour on an eighty-page agreement, forget it—unless you're working for a client for whom every punctuation mark has meaning. In that case, press on. How you provide your services has to fit the context. Perality at work once more.

Let's look at an example from my experience:

Jodie, a third-year associate, took over one of my clients to complete a contract negotiation. Our client was buying a business. The parties had agreed on the basic deal points, and it should have taken no more than a month to get the contract finalized and signed. A great opportunity for a third-year lawyer. Three months later Jodie walked into my office for advice.

"The deal still hasn't closed," she said with a sigh. "We're so far apart on so many issues. The lawyer on the other side is being very difficult. He has an enormous shopping list of problems, which never seem to go away." This is a common refrain: the lawyer from hell on the other side of a deal.

"Out of that enormous list, what are the business issues that our client cares about?" I asked.

"I'm not certain," Jodi answered.

"It's time for you to stop working on this file and go talk to the client. Find out what issues are important, then focus on those points and give in on all the others," I advised.

Three days later the deal closed.

The moral: winning is not about winning every point, just the ones the client cares about. Effective lawyers determine what points are critical to the client and what they can easily concede at low or no cost.

Leverage

Once you've framed your problem, you need to have as much understanding of what the opposing party in a litigation or a negotiation wants to achieve so you can get your clients what they want. What is it you need to give in order to get what you want? How much do you believe they want it, and at what cost? What are they prepared to trade off to get what they want?

Putting yourself in the shoes of the other party is a critical component of framing. Your assessment of the other party may prove to be incorrect, or may have to be adjusted as the matter unfolds, but you need to always keep in mind the objectives of the adverse party. That information is as important to you as what your client wants and at what cost.[18]

Does the other party have greater financial means? Do they have more or less patience than your client? Is your client prepared to wait them out or vice versa? What about the client's ability to manage the stress of an ongoing dispute? How does that weigh against the adverse party? What is the profile of the lawyer on the other side? Are they known to bully their clients to get what they want? How do they measure success? Any intelligence you have on the other party and its counsel is critical.

When advising some of my clients about tax planning options that might be challenged in the future, I always began with the following question: if the Canada Revenue Agency (CRA)[19] began an aggressive audit tomorrow, or if you had to spend ten years in court to prove you were right, how would you sleep at night? If they told me there would be no problem, I would ask the second, more important question. How would your significant other sleep at night? If the answer to either question was unknown or negative, I would advise against the plan.

CRA in most disputes has all the time and most of the leverage. I needed to weed out the clients with anxiety: the extraneous factor that would impact their decision making, regardless of the fact that they would ultimately be proved right. I know many tax lawyers who have not asked those questions and end up with irate clients. Even when the lawyer has given advice that works in theory, the client blames the professional for the predicament. In other words, the stress of the

18. Check out Sun Tzu's *Art of War* if you want to understand the value of intelligence in drawing up your own battle plan. His advice, which was set in a military context, has universal application and is as useful in business as it was when written about 2,500 years ago.

19. Canada's tax collection agency

process is more than the client can bear. A lawyer (or accountant) who doesn't assess how the client will manage that stress has failed!

The final word of advice on leverage comes from Wayne Levin, of Lionsgate:

"I recall one particular discussion with a cable channel (a household name), where I had the leverage to get them to agree to a payment they owed that was three times what they were offering. But that would not have been smart with renewal of our agreement just around the corner, so I settled for something less. And I have to say, that latter negotiation went well after what was viewed as reasonableness on the prior issue. Nothing in business exists in a vacuum."

Which is a great segue into the next point. Clients need to factor in that winning often comes at a price. Are they prepared to pay it? Equally important, are they prepared to pay you as a cost of winning?

> Solving problems in a way that clients get what they can afford and can psychologically deal with is often more important than being right.

Persuasion

Once you've framed the problem, the next task is moving to a solution. You may have worked out the plan of attack, but do you have the confidence to follow it, to face up to the obstacles to achieve your goal?

Ken Atlas refers to a negotiation early in his career as being one of those "turning point moments."

"While still a young lawyer, I had an extended negotiating session with one of Canada's large public companies on the other side. There was a major point of contention. Because the borrower was so large and important, with its choice of lenders, my client, the bank, had very little leverage available, so it was all about convincing the borrower that our position was more reasonable than its position. I spent several hours negotiating the issue opposite various financial officers, sequentially, moving up all the way to the CEO, who (rather quickly) agreed to our position. That was a lesson for me in how to be persuasive. Not being cowed when my convictions were solid."

Ken may have been junior, but the power and conviction of his ideas helped propel him in the early years.

Execution

Mark Le Blanc, general counsel at TVO, expresses the point in a manner applicable to in-house lawyers.

"As counsel, you need to do more than give advice to the business people. You have to make sure that they are capable of executing what they have to do to make the advice worthwhile. That may involve taking them through the process you lay out and showing them how to do it."

Wise advice. In my own experience, it also means checking back in with clients after you've dispensed advice to see if they've implemented it. Many professional firms excel in not only providing the advice, but in training the client's personnel in how to implement the recommendations. The implementation is often a far more valuable part of the process to the client. If you fail to follow up, you're missing out on an important bonding experience with the client.

While this chapter has been dedicated to framing and solving client problems and focusing on the external world and your role in it, the following portion of the book requires an inward turn. As we'll see, the key to your career development is situated between your ears. The psychological issues affecting all of us as professionals can either hold you back or propel you forward. Understanding those issues, and accepting that you can face and overcome them, is critical to your path to success.

PART II

THE PSYCHOLOGY OF SUCCESS

CHAPTER 9

It's All Between Your Ears

Do I take action? Yes or no? Hamlet worded it somewhat differently. "To be or not to be, that is the question." Your entire career will be marked by an endless supply of challenges—forks in the road where you will be tested: which way to go, what risks to take on, what to avoid, and what to embrace.

The choices you make and the ways you manage the psychological issues that you confront will define you and your career path. As you chart your way forward, scaling the biggest mountains standing in your way will not depend on whether you're smart enough, personable enough, learned enough, or ready.

You will never be ready.

You will never have all the necessary qualifications to move on. You will always have to face up to the challenge of finding out whether you can succeed at a new responsibility or task. You will never know in advance whether you will succeed at something new. Understand that the major source of resistance is not coming from the outside. Ultimately, you will cast a glance in the rearview mirror and see the path you carved through the granite of resistance inside your own head.

My three best friends: fear, failure, and risk

Career advancement is married to accepting challenges where failure is a possibility. I don't use the reference to marriage loosely. If you have any hopes of succeeding, you'll be walking down the aisle of your career with the risk of failure at your side. Sometimes you'll be afraid, or you'll be concerned about embarrassment. Or being called out for not yet having the requisite skills, not knowing the answers, or doubting that your answers are correct. When that happens—and it will—don't bolt.

When we begin to work, everything is new, so we have no choice in our level of risk. As one of my professors was wont to remind us, "You have an advantage. Your mind is not yet cluttered with knowledge."[20] Learning is exciting. However, as we become proficient with skills we're developing, we tend to avoid taking on new tasks where we may not succeed. We also tend to hold onto the tasks we have mastered rather than moving on and handing those tasks to more junior people. After all, we can do them faster and more efficiently than the junior staff we could train to take over. That is a mistake.[21]

Leaving the comfort zone

The first major test of my character occurred in my second year of practice. I had written a speech for my boss to deliver, which was then translated from English because he was to give it in French at a major conference in a few days. The morning before the presentation he called the office to advise us that he had contracted chicken pox and was quarantined at home.

A more senior francophone lawyer in the group was asked to replace him, but he replied, "I didn't write it…I can't learn this. I pass." At this point one of the partners in the group asked if I would take it on. I would be speaking in my second language to a group of experts on a subject I had researched in English, but where the technical jargon was all foreign—literally.

Could I sell the elements of an estate plan to a group of experts in

---

20. A posthumous shout-out to professor Paul-André Crépeau, of McGill Law School, for that and other humorous first-year maxims.

21. More about the art of delegation in my next book, *Triple F*.

the field? I knew I would fail as a speaker if I resorted to reading the paper. What could be more boring to an audience! That was my fear. That the audience would be sitting there, falling asleep on me, politely applauding when I was done, not because I was effective, but because it was over. Is there something worse than a performance that's unforgettable because it's that bad?

Still, I said yes.

Might I fall flat on my face? It was possible. I ran home and began to practise in front of the mirror. I figured if I could sell vacuum cleaners in French, what was a little twenty-minute speech? Ha! I didn't sleep very well that night.

The moderator opened with a joke about how the expert who wrote the paper was now presenting it. Luckily the audience thought that was funny.

I could have passed. I could have given in to the fear. The conference could have reduced the panel from three speakers to two. Instead I took the risk. I pushed myself and survived. I learned that I could endure a tough challenge. Some little part of my brain had grown.

And what if I had failed, if the speech had gone poorly?[22] I might be writing today how bouncing back from that personal embarrassment was a challenge I overcame. I might have noted that afterward a senior lawyer came up to me, put his arm around my shoulder, and admitted that it had once happened to him. That he advised me to stay with it. That he admired my courage. That might even be a better life lesson story.

"Failure isn't fatal, but failure to change might be."
— JOHN WOODEN, famous basketball coach for the UCLA Bruins[23]

---

22. Or perhaps it did go badly, but I failed to perceive it that way.

23. Wooden coached the Bruins for twelve years and led them to ten NCAA championships from 1964 to 1975. His nickname was the Wizard of Westwood (the LA district where the campus is located).

We improve by pushing ourselves outside our comfort zone. I cannot tell you how many professionals I know who've been running a limited but economically sufficient practice for the past ten years. They are the known experts at what they do, but they've been doing the exact same thing over and over, every day for years. Is that what you want?

Fernando Garcia, chief in-house counsel at Cargojet, puts it in simple terms: "Take chances. Learn. Continue to be driven by your curiosity and never fear change. We all have to become comfortable with discomfort."

His final point reverberates among all the successful people I interviewed: the only option is to face your fear that you may get it wrong, that you may be criticized, that you may be exposed.

Most of you have succeeded throughout your academic careers. You are used to success. You do not want to fail. You may never have failed…yet. When faced with a new task, our deep-rooted tendency is to avoid failing. And the simplest way to avoid failing is to avoid the task.

"Only those who dare to fail greatly can ever achieve greatly."
— ROBERT F. KENNEDY

Maryse Bertrand, a successful Montreal commercial lawyer who we'll encounter again later, frames it a little differently. "Adversity is opportunity spelled backward," she tells me. I decide not to challenge her on her spelling, but I get the point.

"I used to avoid it," she admits in our interview. "I saw it as terrible. Hard. Adversity made me cry in frustration, made me angry. Early in my career I saw nothing positive in it."

"What changed?" I asked.

"My husband, Bill, a litigator, represented a client in the early days of 'ultimate fighting,' before MMA was popular, when its forerunner was forbidden everywhere for being too violent. His client wanted to stage the fight on an Indigenous reserve, where the federal and provincial laws should not apply. I was concerned the fight might be considered a criminal offence. I thought it was immoral at best. I didn't want him involved. Bill insisted on attending the match in person in case police showed up. Bill is not a criminal lawyer. What did he know about any of this? How could he help the client?"

"That was all subtext for how you really felt?" I asked.

"Mostly I was afraid Bill was getting in over his head with potential violence and bad press. I was scared."

What tipped the balance for Maryse?

"In the middle of our argument, as he was about to leave the house, he said to me, 'If I had only ever done things I knew how to do, I would never be where I am today.' Those words not only won him the argument, but changed my outlook on fear and adversity forever."[24]

"For many of us our proudest achievements come in the face of our greatest adversity."
— MARK MANSON, *The Subtle Art of Not Giving a F*ck*

Riding the emotional roller coaster

When I completed my first year as a lawyer, I was riding high. My reviews were stellar, I was having fun, learning all the time, and writing opinions, research papers, and appeal factums. I was ready for some of my next set of challenges: running small transactions, litigating cases on my own, and applying the tax theory I had learned to particular corporate reorganizations.

Yet within four months my confidence began to sag and I spiralled—in the wrong direction. To this day I cannot explain what happened to me in the second year, but none of it was positive. I had trouble making decisions; I even missed a court filing deadline for an

24. As a matter of history, the evening went off without a hitch, legal or otherwise. These bold promoters paved the road for what would become the new wave of MME that has developed a world-wide following, legitimacy, and regulation.

appeal. If I were my boss, I would have fired me. There were days I woke up worried that someone would figure out I had lost my touch. I had no idea where to begin fixing myself.[25]

I stuck with it, however, and by the start of my third year I could feel myself pulling out of the spiral. Balance was returning to my life. I was one of the lucky ones to emerge without the assistance of counselling, although looking back now I might self-diagnose as having experienced mild depression. I had a healthy marriage and a partner I could discuss these feelings with. I also had a supervising lawyer who looked past my mistakes, saw my potential, and never let me forget it.[26]

The risk of depression doesn't only affect those who feel like they're failing. It can also attack those of us who seem to be on top of our game. By the time I was midway through my fifth year as a lawyer, things had turned so completely around that I knew I was close to partnership in the firm. But deep inside a nagging voice was reminding me that I was not nearly as good as my headlines. That a change in the tax laws in Ottawa could destroy my practice. That at some point the world was going to figure out what I already knew: that my best years were quickly going to fade behind me and I wasn't yet thirty-two. Once the world figured that out, it was only a matter of time until I sank back into the primordial muck and returned to obscurity.

Psychologists call this imposter syndrome.[27] It's the belief that you're not nearly as good as everyone thinks, and at any moment the world will figure it out. It's another way for depression to crawl in and

---

25. In baseball it's known as the "yips." Dodger All Star second baseman Steve Sax went through a period when he could not get the ball to the first baseman. It reached the point where fans held their breath every time he fielded a ground ball. In preparation for an important game, manager Tommy Lasorda went around the club house making sure each player was mentally prepared. He asked one of the players what he thought about when an opposing batter stepped to the plate. The player's answer: "Please don't hit it to Sax."

26. Thank you, Daniel Levinson.

27. If you're looking to dig in on the subject, a good place to start is an excellent 2011 book by Dr. Valerie Young, *The Secret Thoughts of Successful Women: Why Capable People Suffer from the Impostor Syndrome and How to Thrive in Spite of It*. She considers the subgroups of "perfectionist," "superwoman/man," "natural genius," "soloist," and "expert."

create the self-fulfilling prophecy. I walked around with that little voice whispering at me for a few years, until it finally disappeared. I suppose I was one of the lucky ones. In those days, seeking therapy was seen as a sign of weakness, so I chose not to, even though the littlest things would set me off. For example, I cried when I read Dr. Seuss's *Yertl the Turtle* to my children. Talking about these issues is now encouraged by organizations, and dealing with depression, like any other illness, is becoming recognized as a sign of strength.

Even in my most successful years, I faced fears that some of my best ideas might be discredited, that my decisions might prove to be completely wrong, that my best intentions would not be enough, that my answers to questions that had no answers might be wrong. At each of those moments I might have given in to the fear, declared that the risks were not worth taking, and taken no decisions so that I would not be proven wrong. In short, I could have played it safe and stayed with the tried and true, with what I knew. Instead I took risks. Occasionally I fell flat on my face. I failed. I was wrong. But I got up and kept going.

My inner drive pushed me through those moments of doubt along the way. Pushed me past many problems that seemed unsurmountable when I encountered them. But drive alone was not enough to deal with failure and setbacks. I didn't give in, but I did make some colossal errors. Most of those mistakes taught me a heck of a lot more than my successes. I learned to accept that failing would not be the end of the world; that I could pick myself up and keep going; that life would continue, not as I had imagined it, but in an unanticipated way. Those unexpected twists and turns enriched my life, though I can only say that in hindsight.

> *My journey, which appeared to move from success to success, was really a navigation around and through challenges: those where I succeeded and the more useful ones where I failed.*

It would be unusual to go through an entire career without having moments of indecision, mental lapses, and errors. The stress of our outside lives often affects how we carry ourselves in the workplace. There was a time when people didn't dare admit to depression. Times have changed and now the conversation about mental health and depression is no longer hiding in the closet.

Hats off to legal superstars like Supreme Court Justice Clément Gascon, who has openly shared his own career-long battle with depression.[28] Regardless of where we are on the career spectrum, or how successful we appear to be, we are all vulnerable and need to continue to engage in the discussion around mental health.

Are you ready for the next step?

Maryse Bertrand referred me to all kinds of studies about women's advancement in the work force. "We tend to hold ourselves back for promotion on the basis that if we feel the least bit unqualified, we will wait until we master what we need to do before moving forward."

I asked her whether she perceived men differently.

"Men on the other hand will consistently apply for advancement, knowing they are partially unqualified, figuring they will learn what they don't already know from their mistakes. I think women are holding themselves back by something innate that makes us want to be perfect."

It was a habit she had to leave behind in order to move her own career forward.

"Imagine, even late in my career when I was approached to become vice-chair of McGill University, my instinct was to decline. Did I have time for such a position?" Maryse did not wait long before overriding that first instinct. "No man would agonize too much over whether he could manage another position. I recognized that I would figure out how to make it fit and gratefully took the position."

At the end of the day, developing the confidence to "work it out as you go," to make countless mistakes and learn from them, is a key component to advancing your career.

---

28. After his brief disappearance in May 2019, Justice Gascon issued a public statement to the press, stating, "For over twenty years I have been dealing with a sometimes-insidious illness: depression and anxiety disorders."

> *Ultimately, we have to move beyond the insecurity of not being certain we will succeed.*

Jennifer Lee is the global managing partner of client-facing services at Deloitte. Her swift rise over the past twelve years at the organization has been astounding. At the beginning of the COVID-19 pandemic she was called on to coordinate the firm's global client response in over 125 countries. All this while she contemplates the arrival of her forty-second birthday.

Jennifer's parents are Asian immigrants and her father's story is the stuff of novels.[29] I asked Jennifer about the scale and speed of her rise. What is her secret sauce?

"It began as a child, growing up Asian in an all-white community in Belleville. I could never shake the feeling that I was the outsider. It wasn't just skin colour; the clothes never fit me quite right, the makeup was never meant for me, I never fit in. As the outsider I felt compelled to excel at everything." Jennifer took up martial arts as a child, which became more than a hobby, more than an obsession. She joined the Canadian national team in Shotokan karate as a teenager and travelled the world.

"And that has benefitted your career?" I ask.

"I discovered the world had so many shades. That was comforting, though even when in China, then and now, I am reminded that while I look Chinese, I'm not. I speak with an English accent. I will always be the outsider, and as the outsider, I always need to be the best."

That feeling has driven all aspects of Jennifer's life, from personal to family to work.

"Except it also works against me," she confides. "I have to be mindful that as a result I am less likely to take risks."

---

29. At the age of five, Jennifer's father was placed in a rubber tire by his parents in Communist China and swam, on his own, to safety in Hong Kong. From there he eventually made his way to Fiji. Without any formal education he taught himself engineering and English, then emigrated to Canada where he built a career with CN out of Belleville, Ontario.

Of course, when I test that assumption against her career at Deloitte, the facts tell another story.

"I joined Deloitte just as the economic crisis of 2008 set in. For the next dozen years I was too busy trying to survive to think much. It was all gut reaction. More important, I am the child of Asian immigrants.

It's part of my psyche, like so many other first-generation Asian-Canadians. I am still trying to convince myself of the truth. That I'm good enough.

"It is so difficult to let go of the thoughts that drive me sometimes to take on tasks that I should pass up."

I tell her that I assume the fast pace of her rise and success has worked to her career advantage.

"Not every day. I've had some wonderful mentors along the way, but there are both blessings and curses to working in the heart of big business. No shortage of detractors in the upper echelons, people who want to put you in your place, who feel you are a threat to their security and who do what they can to harass and discourage an Asian woman from taking her place in what is still a white man's world. The firm is doing what it can to deal with diversity issues, but privilege has its own power and occasionally uses it to protect itself from 'outsiders.'"

It seems the world of big business has a long way to go on the issue of opening the doors to visible minorities.

Looking at Jennifer's career path objectively, it appears that she has made the doubt work for her at each step along the way.

Surviving mistakes

Matt Diskin is a partner at Dentons Canada LLP and has worked in large firms and a litigation boutique. At age forty he considers himself not yet in his prime as a litigator. "I figure I have another ten years or so until I arrive," he says, and he isn't joking. I asked him if he had ever made a mistake that he considered a turning point moment.

"As a young associate," he told me, "I received a document from a client that he had labelled highly, super confidential. Not to be shared with the other side. The client was completely paranoid about maintaining confidentiality. He was a most difficult client for the partner to manage. No problem. I asked my temporary assistant to transmit a few documents to the adverse party. Wouldn't you know, when I sat down with the paperwork that had been sent out, I discovered that the confidential paper had made its way into the pile.

"She should have noticed the notation on the document that the client had added: 'Not to be sent.' She didn't. I could have blamed her. Except *she* had not received the instruction. I did. Had I double-checked my assistant's work I would have caught it, but it never occurred to me this document was in the pile.

"I was sick to my stomach. After a couple of minutes, I knew what I had to do. I summoned my courage, walked into the partner's office, and admitted *my* error. Not *my assistant's* error. I will never forget just how inadequate I felt at that moment. Ultimately the situation resolved, and I learned my lesson. Not that I should never trust anyone working for me, but that if I ever made another mistake—and there have been a number along the road to partnership—I had to deal with it immediately and take personal responsibility."

> *Reporting an error you make on a file is a test of your character.*

Hoping it will go away on its own, pretending you're not responsible, or finding someone else to take the blame are all failures of your fortitude.

There isn't a single one of us who has not exercised poor judgment or otherwise erred at some point in our career. In our lives![30] If you want to see a complete manual on mistakes, speak to any leader.

Even managing partners get it wrong about 25 percent of the time.

They will tell you that their success isn't negated by their mistakes; rather their success is determined by how well and how swiftly they deal

---

30. As a lawyer with over thirty years' experience, I made the exact same mistake as Matt. It was for a client from hell. It took a few days until my hearing returned.

with the mistakes, and the lessons for the future that they derive from them. Leaders understand that we learn far more from our mistakes (tough as they are to swallow) than from our immediate successes.

The true test of a professional is not whether you never make a mistake—you most certainly will—but rather how you deal with the mistake once you discover it. That will define the content of your character.

Building resilience

Dr. Larry Richard is an organizational psychologist and lawyer who has studied well over ten thousand lawyers and how they compare with the general population. It might surprise you to know that, statistically, this group of professionals, who make a living engaging in confrontation, generally score well below the mean population in their ability to accept criticism and in resilience, which Dr. Richard defines in our interview as "how thick- or thin-skinned one is in the face of criticism or rejection."[31]

If you want to understand the issue in more depth, here is an excellent podcast:
shows.acast.com/hpleadershippodcast/episodes/5a6122a1c392 708165a467cb

This general weakness in resilience might explain why lawyers avoid situations where they may fail and dodge new tasks that leave them open to criticism. Surprisingly, though, as Dr. Richard explains, resilience can be built, whether in your working life or in your personal life.

"Engaging in positive conversations with people you know and trust for as little as five minutes a day has demonstrated a general improvement in one's attitude and in the ability to deal with the curveballs that life throws at us."

---

31. If you would like to hear Dr. Richard on other issues, you can check out his website http://lawyerbrain.com/

On the value of self-talk to improve resilience, check out this podcast:
Talkabouttalk.com/26-self-talk-with-dr-andrea-wojnicki

A Harvard Business review article[32] suggests that the degree of optimism we bring to our daily challenges, including the ones where we stumble and fall, will affect how we respond to a setback. How does that apply in a profession where, according to Dr. Richard, we far outscore the mean population in terms of cynicism and skepticism?

On average we are not the most optimistic bunch! Dr. Richard's statistics confirm that. But the purpose of this section is not to suggest you try increasing your own natural level of optimism. Rather it's to point out that if you resist challenges out of fear, you'll be holding yourself back and limiting your career development. Recognizing that as lawyers our brains appear to be more naturally wired to resist criticism helps us understand why we also resist trying new experiences and testing our limits.

For a great podcast on resilience with a popular personality, check out
Talkabouttalk.com/25-building-resilience-with-tosca-reno

Grit or talent: which matters more?

This next section might not win me any popularity points, because there is no easy path to success on any professional path. Your success will be a function of your determination. Your power to persevere. Your grit.

Psychologist Angela Duckworth[33] has found that the greatest predictor of success among students is their grit, which she defines as perseverance to set and pursue long-term goals. She points out that

32. https://bit.ly/39FJRck Building Resilience, Martin E.P. Seligman, April 2011
33. Check out her book, *Grit: the Power of Passion and Perseverance*, if you want the long version, or her TED Talk https://bit.ly/3i2YWbv for a six-minute summation of her findings. Interestingly enough she can explain the phenomenon but not the reasons.

many talented individuals simply do not follow through on their commitments. According to her data, grit is often unrelated to or even inversely related to measures of talent. Translation: your determination will be a greater predictor of success than your natural talent. This means if you can bear down, apply the lessons, and not give up, you are more likely to outperform more naturally gifted competitors.

Your career is a marathon rather than a sprint. There will be intense bouts of pain that you have to fight through, mountains of doubt that you need to overcome. Relying on your grit to carry you through those times is paramount. Setting long-term goals and never wavering is a better strategy than relying only on your talent. Occasionally you will achieve the "runner's high" and feel that you can coast forever. Those periods of intense productivity and success will inevitably be followed by new uphill challenges, where you need to call on your grit, once more, in order to evolve.

This might be the most important point I make in this book:

Your success is not going to be predicted by your talent.

Top of class, middle of class, natural learner, library studier—all only partly relevant. There is something far more important at play:

> *Your determination to set goals and pursue them, even if it takes years, will define your success.*

As a final story, Justice Lori Anne Thomas, the recently appointed judge we met in Chapter 6, is the daughter of a single mother who struggled with mental illness. She was an underprivileged child who went to work after high school and studied for her undergraduate degree at night and through correspondence courses. She was admitted to law school at thirty years old. She tells me that she considered herself one of the "privileged class," despite her start in life, although when her mother died in the middle of Lori Anne's second year, it was crushing.

"I considered withdrawing for six months to pull myself together. Most of my social network supported me, though one friend took a risk and confronted me. He bluntly told me that he considered a six-month leave of absence to be grieving on my own a complete waste of my time—that [it] wouldn't help me at all. It was a callous remark that hurt. However, once I got over my shock, I gave some thought to his comment and came to see he was right. I put my head down and kept going."

Justice Thomas's case poignantly illustrates that sometimes we need to rely on people around us to help find our grit and move forward through the pain—even the pain of loss—and carry on.

Time management: choices

Perhaps the single most critical issue driving young professionals away from private practice is the issue of how to balance career development with a life outside of work. I am a firm proponent of the advice that Peter Blaikie spouted to all of our lawyers. I paraphrase: You are worth far less to your client as a one-dimensional lawyer who only has time for the law, than as a well-rounded, well-read professional who has developed outside interests. Those other interests will contribute to your developing perspective on dealing with people and their problems.

But how do you balance that goal against meeting the time requirements of private practice, billing enough hours to meet your quota, marketing, building for the future, writing, speaking, managing a family life (if you have or want one), and controlling your own destiny, while still finding it exciting to get up every morning for the challenges that await?

I wish I could tell you there's a panacea that allows you to have a life while you're practising law, or any other profession, but each of you will have to determine what guides your choices.

I asked Maryse Bertrand about this issue, particularly as it relates to women lawyers trying to balance career and family.[34] Maryse is one

---

34. We still haven't reached the point where men can be uniformly counted on to take 50 percent of the responsibility for child-rearing.

of Montreal's most successful commercial lawyers, specializing in capital markets and acquisitions. She was a partner in a major law firm and left to join the CBC as a senior executive. She now sits on the board of a number of Quebec's most dynamic companies and, as mentioned earlier, is the vice chair of McGill University. I first met Maryse on her first day of law school in 1977; as a second-year student I was leading a tour for the rookies. We were nobodies with unformed aspirations.

"Perfection is overrated," she tells me in a matter-of-fact tone, early in the interview. "As women we are brought up with this genetic code, telling us if we are going to do something, we have to be perfect. If you try and apply that to every phase of your life, you are going to go crazy."

So, what is the secret of managing time?

"Simple," she says. "Accept that there will be compromises. You can't have everything. You can't be everywhere. Spouse, kids, clients…. Everyone is going to get a little shortchanged. Some of the balls you are juggling will drop."

And that's OK?

"It's more than OK. It's human. I had to make decisions between client dinners and dance recitals. The recitals won. My choice. I couldn't be everywhere for work like my male partners.[35] I accepted it and clients accepted it. *I made my priorities and lived with them.* But I was not the 'make-lunch-for-tomorrow mother,' not the 'carpool mother.' I decided what was important to *me* and I lived with it. My kids learned to understand the trade-offs. It made them stronger. They eventually appreciated that I knew what counted. All of that made me a happier person."

Jennifer Lee, a partner at Deloitte, is among the most creative career women I have had the privilege to meet. A mother of two young sons,

35. Is the pendulum swinging from where it was when Maryse was building a family and it was unthinkable that the male partner would have to make the choices that women had to make decades ago? In 2020 we are seeing somewhat more balance and more male professionals engaging in the same debate.

she points out that early in her marriage, her husband was the principal bread winner, but as she advanced to a global position at her firm, the reverse was becoming true. The couple adapted its lifestyle, but to manage her young family she came up with a creative solution to the 40 percent of her time spent travelling around the world.

"Rather than disappear for a month at a time, I would use my travel budget to take my entire family along, whether to Germany, Japan, or Singapore. I took my business class ticket and fancy hotel and traded it for economy for all of us and a cheaper rental. In Germany much of my work was remote, so I was able to spend more face time with the family and we made arrangements for the kids to be locally educated on the trips that were up to a month at a time. Strange that I never felt comfortable admitting this until this interview!"

The boys, now aged eleven and eight, speak four languages and think nothing of it.

"We had to be very flexible to keep it all together and it cost us an economic fortune, but my priority was my family, and this crazy plan actually worked, because the kids were young enough at the time. One child celebrated a birthday in Japan, the other in China. The only disappointment—missing Halloween."

André Bacchus is one of the founders of the Law Practice Program at Ryerson University and a true pioneer in diversity and developing young legal talent. André is well known in legal circles in Ontario. I asked him how he got there.

"I was travelling in the fast lane, a third-year associate at Fried Frank in New York City, with a big salary, growing responsibilities, and a lucrative future as a securities lawyer at the 'financial centre of the universe.' Of course, the fast lane meant no time for socializing, work to all hours of the night, client demands that were only growing. No time for me.

"My lasting image of that time was walking near the FDR highway immediately after 9/11. Friends and strangers ambling alongside a deserted highway that runs from the financial district all the way up Manhattan. It was a ghost town, kind of like Toronto in the midst of COVID-19. Kind of like the void in my life.

"The little voice in my head was telling me there had to be more than this. The career path was a tempting lure, but is this what I really wanted? I felt no passion for it, but should that matter? I was *on track*. But on track for what? I needed time to think. The firm gave me a month leave, and when I returned, I understood what I had to do."

"So," I asked, "you didn't think the big salary, annual bonus, and potential partnership were enough to create a passion?"

"It was probably the hardest decision of my life, but I decided to walk away. I returned to Toronto. But not to that life. I slowly discovered that with my interest in people, I belonged in recruiting. I found a job recruiting as part of a team—building an associates' program at a progressive and growing firm. Eventually they asked me to build and run that program. I was never more inspired in my life. And then for reasons outside my control, I had to move on. When I was approached with the Ryerson opportunity, I was certain it was for me.

"I am thrilled with my life. I stay in touch with my former colleagues in New York. I don't care how much money they're making. I'm happy. My husband's happy. My life is in balance."

André's words of advice to young professionals:

"Follow your passion. It takes courage to leave what you know, even if it's not making you unhappy. But ask and continue to ask whether it's fulfilling you. If not, look hard within. More than anything else, don't let the fear of making a decision paralyze you."

Andre's ongoing evolution has brought him to the newest chapter and next challenge in his own life. He is the director, Career Development & Professional Placement Office, at the newly created faculty of law at Ryerson which opened in 2020.

The relationship between fighting fear and following the voice in your head is the subject of the next chapter.

CHAPTER 10

Learning What Works for You

Myriad factors can influence your career. Some of them are within your control, and others may be chalked up to luck, to being in the right place at the right time, or to staying the course at a particular career crossroad. How do you make decisions along the way?

The lessons of Uncle Harry

My Uncle Harry was a renowned Montreal pediatrician who treated a generation of boomers (literally while they were babies!) He was also awarded the Order of the British Empire for initiating the inoculation of Canadian troops headed for the WW2 theatre. It was a radical idea in the early 1940s. On his deathbed Uncle Harry gave me two pieces of advice:

- Whatever you do for a living, make sure you love it.

- Your career is a river. Save your energy and find the current, then follow it.

At age nineteen I had no way of appreciating Uncle Harry's wisdom. I only appreciated the advice thirty years later when I looked back and saw that I had actually followed it. So how do I make this advice practical for you so that you can actually take it and use it?

Early in your career: explore

One of the best restructuring lawyers I ever had the chance to work with was Ken Atlas, whom you first met in Chapter 1. For the first three years of practice he split his work between litigation and transactional matters. After a period of time, litigation began to lose its appeal. He found that the highs of winning were too high and the lows of losing were too low.

"That's the way my brain is built," Ken tells me. "Maybe I like winning too much." The outcomes of the cases depended on a judge's decision, which Ken could not control. Winning or losing didn't correlate with the amount of effort he put in. It took a psychological toll.

"I decided to refocus my practice on commercial transactions, drafting and negotiating contracts. I found that my litigation experience in recovery matters gave me a good perspective to work on bank financing matters, as I fully understood what was essential in an agreement and how a court would see any breach. I started to do work on secured financings for bank clients, and eventually I worked on some sophisticated financings for some of our bank clients. I was in love. I found that my ability to persuade opposing counsel or their client of the reasonableness of my position far exceeded my ability to persuade a judge of, well, virtually anything."

Did Ken's early years in litigation set the stage for his success as a transaction lawyer? According to him, most certainly. When he began litigating, did he have the slightest notion that he might become a leading banking lawyer? Not a chance.

Daniel Lo's current situation may be more in line with your own plan to move around and experiment in the first few years of your career. Daniel was born in Hong Kong and grew up in Mississauga, Ontario. He did his law school in Birmingham, England, completed the final stage of his solicitor training course in London, and then decided to return to Canada. It was just after the financial crisis of 2008: not a job to be found, and he still had to qualify in Ontario. Undaunted, he did a masters at U of T, found a job at RBC Capital Markets, and eventually moved to Dentons' office in Calgary.

The voice in the back of his head then returned him to his roots in Hong Kong, where he slept on the floor of his grandmother's apartment for four months until finding work with a private equity firm and got some in-house legal experience. When his fiancée was accepted to do an MBA in Singapore, he jumped at the challenge and found a job with Walkers, an international offshore law firm. During the COVID-19 pandemic, as I write this, Daniel works virtually in his new environment within the asset management arm of UBS.

"I've been tested by uncertain job markets, unemployment, a cold hard floor, and most recently by my first opinion to some business managers, who told me that my decision 'had better be right,' as it affected a multi-million-dollar financial asset transaction. In-house you learn very quickly that risk assessment and confident decision making are essential skills."

In terms of what's coming next for Daniel, he's not worried. He has been listening to his inner voice and following his river. Who knows? It might bring him back one day to Toronto.

The point is, your career experiences, whether you like them or not, establish a foundation on which you can build once you've found the area of practice that turns your crank later on.

Follow the river

So many experts advise you to "follow your passion." Early in your career that advice is worthless. Of the people I've interviewed, guess how many experienced success in an area they targeted at the start of their career? NONE. They will tell you, to a person, that they have all followed Uncle Harry's second rule. They followed the river, keeping a keen eye out for opportunities that presented themselves along the way.

Uncle Harry graduated from medical school certain he was going into obstetrics, his passion. However, there were no jobs in that field. Instead he was offered a position in pediatrics, which he took. The rest is history.

If he'd just taken the advice to follow his passion, he may well have waited for the right position and found himself unemployed, missing out on an incredibly rich career. A career that he loved. A career he felt no passion for when he began! But he followed the river until he found the current.

Similarly, I have found that the parts of my career that I loved the most and that gave me the most satisfaction were those that I could never have predicted. While I was certain I wanted to be a tax lawyer, I had no idea until my fifth year of practice that I might become a film finance specialist. At the start it was not particularly lucrative. The Canadian film industry was young, so I found only a smattering of work to fill some gaps in my schedule.[36] I discovered that the further I explored, though, the more I enjoyed the work, and clients began to find me.

Uncle Harry's second rule is poetic. Your career is not a series of straight lines from job to job. It is a river that turns, changes directions, and has a current. You have a choice in managing your career. At times, having charted a direction that is upstream, you'll feel like you're fighting the current, which is sapping your energy while you chase an elusive goal. The other choice is to simply follow the current, taking the opportunities that present themselves along the way. You will expend far less energy and may get to a much better place—one you could not possibly have imagined.

For Uncle Harry it meant giving up his dream to become an obstetrician and taking the opening in pediatrics, which shaped his career. For me it was saying yes, rather than no, to unexpected ideas and possibilities when I had no idea whether I could succeed.

I rarely, if ever, say no—particularly when it comes to something where I lack the requisite skills. I spent years rewiring myself to say yes, even when the voice of doubt whispered at the back of my head.

---

36. I must admit, those early days were wild. One of my clients was a film promoter nicknamed the Rabbi, because he was an actual rabbi in Winnipeg. Many of the film production companies lived hand to mouth and lied to everyone about everything, particularly their financial capacity to produce films. Denis Héroux, a famous Montreal producer, taught me that financing a movie is like filling the last seats on a train. All you need is the last-second passengers (the final investors still not certain if they're going to climb aboard or wait for the next opportunity) reaching for something to grab onto as the train pulls out of the station.

I learned to quiet that doubt by investing the time to learn how to do the job.

Jennifer Pollock, VP of finance and operations for Ratehub.ca (a personal finance company helping Canadians make more informed financial decisions) describes her journey. "The path that led me to where I am was totally unpredictable. While in business school I was late choosing accounting to qualify for on-campus interviews for the Big Four accounting firms, so I ended up at a mid-size firm. In hindsight I found the experience more in tune with what I needed. Less rigidity and more hands-on client experience. They even sent me on a secondment to Los Angeles. Nothing ever worked out the way I expected. It worked out better. I also learned the value of teamwork,[37] a critical component of my current job."

I'm not suggesting that every decision you make will pay immediate dividends. In my third year of practice, the person who was feeding me most of my tax work went through a nasty divorce. There was little work for me to do. One of the more senior lawyers remembered that while I was working my way through law school, I spent a couple of years learning how to do real estate title searches.

The firm had been asked to handle some real estate transactions for a few new clients, and it seemed that I had the most expertise of anyone in the firm in this area. Even though I had sworn years earlier I would never do another title search, I agreed and was "redeployed." Almost two years later I was emerging as the leader of the real estate group, an area of law in which I had no interest. Where were the tax files I had come to love? Should I be leaving for something else? I was really good at and respected for a skill that I myself had no respect for. Irony theatre.

I toughed it out, largely as a result of the confidence the firm had shown in me earlier in my practice. I was following Uncle Harry's river, though I still had no idea that it was slowly transporting me toward an experiment in film finance that would change my life forever, and where I would find my true passion.

---

37. More on the critical value of following and leading teams in my next book, *Triple F.*

Keep your options open

I've heard stories about the recent pressures on students to declare their practice interests while in first or second year or in advance of OCIs. To say that is both unrealistic and unnatural might be the understatement of the year. How can you possibly know what practice area will interest you based on some coursework? If you must do this to survive OCIs, then play the game, but remember to keep your options open for as long as you can. Few students know yet how or when their passion will develop or where the current of their career will take them. In the future you may retain the same basic values, but your experience, skill development, and psychological adjustments will change you in ways you cannot yet imagine. Here are some examples:

André Bacchus walked away from a lucrative career as a Manhattan securities lawyer and found a job more suited to him developing young professionals in Toronto.

Erin O'Toole, leader of the Conservative Party of Canada, practised law until he succumbed to the voice in his head to follow in his father's footsteps to serve the public good as a member of Parliament. As a former soldier (twelve years in the armed forces), he was also a founder of True Patriot Love, a charity whose mission is to inspire Canadians to contribute to the resilience of military and veteran families.

Erin is a big believer in orientation. "Most important, choose a work environment consistent with what is important to you. For me it was social justice."

Mark Le Blanc was practising at an intellectual property boutique when the chance to move in-house at CBC presented itself. It turned out to be a wise move a few years later when the GC position at TVO arose. Mark now leads a group that has been part of a corporate transformation, testing his legal and business skills.

There are countless cases of lawyers who like their work environment but don't enjoy what they're doing. Lorene Nagata is one of the leading head hunters in the country. She runs

NagataConnex out of her office in Toronto. She began her career as a litigator in a mid-size firm, and when she realized after more than four years in practice that she was not having fun, she called a search firm to help find her something else. After a few meetings they concluded she might be best suited to recruiting rather than law. That was the start of a fruitful career, which later saw her branch off to begin her own business. A leap of faith—into herself. She had a unique take on her situation when she made that jump.

"For a number of years, I was one of the few women business owners in an alpha male world. I saw that as a distinct advantage."

Don't lose your balance

Are you in the right environment to find your balance? Part of this can be answered by examining whether you're aligned with the values of the place you work. I'm not talking about the firm's stated values or principles, but rather the actions of the firm that demonstrate those values.

Is someone going to pat you on the back and pay you a fat bonus for docketing over 2,200 hours in the year? It means you're a lucrative asset. If you see that as a badge of honour advancing your career, then you are at the right place. If you're exhausted and burning out and not a soul is noticing, or if you can't remember the name of your second child, then perhaps you're not aligned with your firm. More likely you're a step away from leaving the practice.

On the other hand, if you're at a firm where a senior professional will tell you that your life is out of balance and sit down and talk to you about off-loading some of your work, then you are likely at the right place.

Understanding that periods of intense work are normal, but that unabating periods of stress will deplete you, is an important part of self-monitoring. Building time into your calendar to spend with your family and friends, or engaging in activities outside the practice, is both normal and healthy. However, if you're in a firm where all the partners are working until eight at night and you walk out at four to attend your yoga class, followed by dinner with the family and a movie, you may not be at the right place for you.

As firms adopt "mindfulness" as part of their mantra, you will have to decide for yourself whether they are paying lip service to the notion, or whether they are set up in daily practice to deal with the issues of mental health that dog the professional industry. In this regard I am speaking not just about the literature they publish or the programs the administrators roll out. I mean whether the owners of the firm are really committed to the principle, based on the way they behave and their expectations.

So many young professionals understand this and are moving toward in-house, practising out of their home office, or accepting other jobs more suited to their own goals. My only caveat here is that in-house positions, other than at certain institutional clients, can be just as intense as private practice. Do your homework before you move. Also recognize that working in a diverse (or even political) environment early in your career will teach you about teamwork and managing politics. It can be worth sucking it up for a few years to learn some valuable practical lessons in dealing with people (some of them rather difficult).

There will be times when things feel out of balance. Occasionally the imbalance may go on for months. The key is to weigh what is important to you over the long term, recognizing that in order to advance there are going to be periods of intense stress and adjustment. But you owe it to yourself to make sure your resources are replenished and that your sacrifices for work are not permanent. According to Dr. Julie McCarthy, professor of organizational behaviour and human resource management in the Department of Management at University of Toronto, this means that if you break away from work to spend time with family, to exercise, or to socialize, don't bring the office problems along with you.[38] Some professionals believe they should completely wall off everything at

38. See for example, McCarthy, J.M. (2020). *How to Take Control of Your Well-Being.* Rotman Magazine, 4, 96–98

work from their home and social lives. However, studies show that there is a benefit to sharing positive work experiences with family and friends.[39]

I've heard the following anecdote told in various versions from senior professionals complaining about what they label "the new work ethic." A call comes in at four in the afternoon. The client needs advice by noon tomorrow. It's an emergency that will require someone to research, write, and have ready a polished presentation in eighteen hours. (You may believe that all-nighters are only a part of the university cramming experience. Realistically it happens more often in practice than you might expect.) The senior partner walks in and asks for your assistance. Except it's date night with your significant other. What to do? What do you choose? Who was it who said, "We are the product of our choices"?[40]

Banking on your talents

How much do education and background count for success? Some people seem to have all the advantages going into their career: growing up in the "right" circle, acing all their courses, and/or having the winning personality that naturally attracts people. But even if you were a mediocre student, come from a challenged background, or have few, if any, connections at this point in your career, success can still be yours.

---

39. According to Dr. McCarthy, while it's always a good idea to create a solid boundary between negative events that happen at work and your home life, it is also important to allow the positive events and emotions to spill over from work to home (and vice versa). In the academic literature this is labelled "work-to-life facilitation" (as opposed to work-to-life conflict), and it is a relatively new research area that shows how important it is to take the positive things and allow them to enter our personal lives—by sharing positive work news and stories, and recognizing and thinking about positive work events. See also, Heskiau, R., & McCarthy, J. M. (2020). *A work–family enrichment intervention: Transferring resources across life domains.* Journal of Applied Psychology.

40. Stephen R. Covey deals with the issue in his book, *The 7 Habits of Highly Effective People.*

Here's a wonderful example. Fernando Garcia is the son of Latin American immigrants, blue-collar workers who raised him in the Jane-Finch corridor, one of Toronto's toughest and most diverse neighbourhoods.

"I wasn't much of a student in high school," he readily admits. "I barely scraped by with a below-C average. I went through five different schools, suffered from attention deficit, and I never fit the academic mould. The only thing I liked about school was the social dynamic."

Not exactly the background that would predict legal career success, but today he is among Toronto's prominent in-house counsels and a local champion of diversity.

"I'm living proof that the guy from the bottom of the class can make it." I smile just listening to Fernando. Perhaps it's his gift; he's so natural. He doesn't sound polished. What you see is what you get with Fernando, and he has turned that into a career advantage.

"I grew up in a diverse neighbourhood like so many new Canadians. That's why I feel it's so important that we see ourselves as Canadians first, without regard to our external differences. I'd rather focus on the values that unite us."

It all sounds very patriotic, but Fernando lives and breathes passion for his career. How does he explain the turnaround from mediocre student to successful lawyer?

"When I was finally ready to get serious about my life, I discovered that self-directed learning was more positive than the classroom. Then I connected with subject matter that really appealed to me—politics, labour relations, sociology—which led to a master's in labour relations until I finally found my way to law. After I graduated and found an in-house position, I was able to do an executive MBA."

Fernando learned that giving legal advice could not be divorced from understanding the business issues, and in that regard the business education came in handy. Over time, understanding what made people tick was also critical.

Fernando's key piece of advice:

"Be curious your entire career. You need to want to learn."

He sees his upbringing as a career advantage. He has always been comfortable with people of diverse backgrounds and economic status, which has been a huge help in his work for international companies such as Navistar and, later, Nissan. When he started at Navistar, he was just two years from his call.

"Did I have any idea what I could offer? No, but I was able to contribute and grow my skill sets, even taking on the role of director of HR along with the GC role."

Years ago, when he began at Nissan, the company was looking to substantially expand its Canadian market share. He joined an international team whose mission was to re-establish the brand. A true interdisciplinary skill set and cooperation were required. The initiative was a success.

"At the start of each job I was uncomfortable, thrown in to situations for which I had little to no experience. Slowly I learned that my social skills, my life training of getting along with people in Jane-Finch from all over the world, was an asset."

Diversity challenges

Wes Hall, who has taken the lead in organizing and promoting the 2020 BlackNorth Initiative,[41] has achieved an incredible amount in the thirty-five years since he arrived in Canada in 1985 as a sixteen-year-old immigrant from Jamaica. He caught my attention many years ago when he began successfully competing with major trust companies for the business of large Canadian corporations to handle their shareholder relations. The proverbial David battling the Goliaths of the business. How did Wes make the climb?

"When people ask how I've overcome adversity in my career," he tells me as we begin the interview, "I take out a picture of me and my grandma in front of her tin shack in Jamaica. That was my life before I emigrated. We had nothing.

41. The BlackNorth Initiative was created to recruit CEOs across Canada to combat systemic racism in corporate Canada. Further information can be found at their website, https://blacknorth.ca/Home.

"When I arrived in Canada I went to live with my father in Malvern." I shake my head. Malvern is one of the toughest neighbourhoods in the northeast of Toronto. For a number of years my law firm ran an outreach program there to help high school graduates into the workforce. Gang violence and drugs contribute to the challenge of survival and success.

"After what I came from in Jamaica," he tells me, "this was paradise. A house with a real roof. I never saw it as run down. I also could not imagine the luxury neighbourhoods of Toronto from where I was growing up a teenager. I had no basis of comparison and I felt fortunate. I considered myself the luckiest kid on earth to be out of a life that led nowhere in Jamaica. It's all about perspective."

How did Wes make it out and become successful?

"If you don't put any limitations on yourself, the sky's the limit. That is the beginning and the end of my philosophy. But that's not how I started. Like everyone else, I had all kinds of doubts about myself and my abilities. The big surprise was that a lot of people I met along the way believed in me. I doubted myself but I needed to prove *them* right about their belief in me. I also had to learn to ignore the voices of the well-meaning skeptics. The people with credibility who raised doubts about my ideas."

"In other words," I ask him, "not every well-meaning piece of advice should be taken at face value?"

"No," he responds without hesitation. *"Beware the well-meaning people who talk you out of your dreams. There is no room for doubt if you want to succeed."*

I ask Wes what drove him to spearhead BlackNorth. "It was an idea whose time had arrived. If I didn't run with it, who would? Once again, I didn't hesitate. People are telling me that getting corporate Canada to finally take action on achieving diversity in the C-suite and in boardrooms of our public companies has always been a losing proposition. That is exactly why I took it on. It's time to prove everyone wrong.

"I have an obligation to my community to take on another great challenge, and I know it will succeed if I can convince our supporters of the power of our ideals."

What worked for Wes and what continues to work for him is turning the challenge of diversity into a sword to carve his way through his career.

When you reach the split in the river, take it.[42]

Christina Porretta has just taken on the job of general counsel at BDO Canada LLP, a major accounting and consulting firm. Her career path involved all kinds of choices along the way. Raised in a strict Italian family, she's the eldest of three girls and was the first to move away from home—to attend law school at the University of Windsor. During the second-year recruitment process, Christina's first-year marks were not sufficient to get her to Bay Street, but she was grateful to be hired as a summer student at the Hamilton office of a major law firm. Christina's academic performance improved considerably in her second and third years of law school, which allowed her to obtain a clerkship at the Federal Court of Appeal.

Following her clerkship, she spent a couple of years litigating at a Bay Street firm and then left to pursue a master's degree. Part of her soul-searching suggested to her that while she loved doing research and drafting arguments on complex issues, she did not enjoy the fact-finding/evidence aspect of litigation. Solution? A research lawyer position back on Bay Street.

"It was the perfect job for me," she tells me in our interview. "I worked with various practice groups on all kinds of issues I found interesting and kept learning. The firm was very supportive all along and appreciated my contributions so much that eventually I became a partner, even though my practice did not require me to have a book of business.

"I felt I needed to stretch some more and was appointed chair of the student committee. That tested all kinds of new leadership skills, including spearheading changes to the firm's recruitment strategy and

---

42. Uncle Harry's take on the line coined by New York Yankees manager Yogi Berra. "When you reach the fork in the road, take it."

the students' professional development curriculum. I suggested a re-orientation that I had to sell internally, orchestrate, and implement. It was challenging but worthwhile.

"I wasn't looking for new challenges, but when I was approached by BDO I had to ask myself some tough questions. I had been a research lawyer for almost ten years, and felt as though I had plateaued. Could I see myself doing research until retirement?"

Christina then asked herself the same question that so many of us ask at the key turning point moments of our careers.

If not now, then when, if ever?[43]

"The notion of leaving the safety and comfort of partnership in an environment where I was valued was daunting. I was scared. I had never imagined going in-house. But I also knew if I did not take this next challenge, I would be giving up an opportunity to develop new skills and to grow as a lawyer."

BDO wanted to build "the in-house legal department of the future." What did Christina know about that?

"As a research expert I was trained at figuring things out." Christina sees that skill as critical in approaching the new challenges in designing the legal department of the future. Christina is invigorated and happy. Her final words of advice: ***"Do what makes you happy and you'll end up at the right place."***

Are we there yet?

We all know this question, which children ask on long journeys.[44] Is it applicable to us as professionals? Do you ever reach your destination on your boat ride on Uncle Harry's river?

43. Christina's quote reminds me of a famous two thousand year old proverb, coined by theologian Hillel, "If I am not for me, then who will be, and if I am only for me, then what am I? And if not now, then when?"
44. The question is timeless. For my children, it began twenty minutes after I pulled the car out of the driveway. My late father would have made the same comment about me.

This is an intriguing question. The short answer: it's completely up to you. Sometimes the river bends to the place you see as home. Will it be permanent? That depends in part on how happy you are with where you've arrived, and in part on luck and circumstances beyond your control. I settled into a managing partner role for fifteen years at a firm I knew to be home. One year after my term as managing partner ended, the firm collapsed and my journey began once more.

But during those fifteen years there were challenges that had to be navigated, some of them existential. I loved every moment—moments when I worried, laughed, and cried, and even those moments when I struggled and wasn't sure I'd succeed. I learned in those years that I had to accept the current, but I also had to keep steering my career boat.

There are more stories I'll recount, all different on their face, yet all sharing the common thread of facing a moment of decision, testing the current, and deciding whether to stay or move on. These stories will appear in the following chapters.

But for now, the next portion of the book will focus on skill-set development.

PART III

DAILY PRACTICE OF SUCCESS

CHAPTER 11

Basic Skills for Expanding Your Practice

In order to expand your practice, you need to develop various skill sets. The prerequisite for getting started in this chapter is that you have one client. That's right. One client relationship is all you need to begin building. For those of you in firms where more senior people "control the client," don't worry. You still qualify!

Unless you're the smartest professional in the firm, or in the rare situation where you have a mentor who's about to retire and wants to transfer all her files to you, at some point you're going to have to step up and build your practice. Better to start developing now. You don't have a moment to lose.

But how do you do it? How do you go from being just another service professional, as fungible as the dollar bills in the client's wallet, to someone a prospective client calls on regularly? How do you get more business?

Many associates sit behind their desks for years—expecting partnership to find them there eventually—wondering what's going to happen next to increase their client range and base. No one has spent any time training them for the big moment when they have to become responsible to themselves. It's as if they expect a fairy godmother to wave a wand and start them on the next stage of their tale. You don't want that to be you.

As I mentioned previously, becoming a respected advisor is all about understanding clients and showing them why they are the most important people in your life. The one piece of advice that every consultant is unanimous about is this:

An existing client is a far more reliable source of new business than a potential client.

The hard work of building the trust has been done, and the potential returns are considerably higher. Whether you're a young lawyer or an experienced one, the easiest place to begin marketing is with your existing clients.

And whether you're at a small firm, a large firm, or on your own, there are steps you can take to begin the process of becoming independent and successful. The longer you wait, the more you rely on others to feed you bits and pieces of work, and the more vulnerable you become.

Let's break the process down into these digestible steps:

- Get in front of clients and overcome your fear of talking to them.

- Distinguish yourself with your work.

- Market yourself in a way that's suited to you.

- Network, and take advantage of mentorship and sponsorship.

It begins with the client visit

Your first encounter with a client will often be in your office. So many professionals assume that's where you should meet a client. That's a bad assumption and can be bad business, because your office closes you off to what lies beyond.

Instead, go visit your client at their place of business. I learned this the easy way when I was still based in Montreal and decided to try expanding my client base into Toronto. Twice a month I would get on a plane in the morning and visit two or three film studios across Toronto over the course of the day. One or two were clients I had been serving from my base in Montreal, while the third would be a prospect. On the first visit I would meet my key contact. Invariably I would get a tour of the offices. That would allow me to see how their organization was set up physically. It also involved introductions to some of the other personnel.

On second and third visits the magic began to happen. I would come to meet about a particular agenda. A few additional people would be called into the meetings because they were in the building and could step in for a few minutes to provide their input on the matter at hand. I found out more about them and what other matters they were working on—not in order to get more immediate work, but as a matter of curiosity and interest. My contacts expanded beyond just the in-house lawyer to the wider business team. More importantly, clients were genuinely touched that I made the effort to come see them: that I invested the time commuting and was demonstrating genuine interest, just by showing up.

What I did not realize at the time was that all these meetings and additional connections showed my clients that I cared about their business. None of their other lawyers were doing this. Very often the clients' auditors would be in the middle of an audit. Sometimes they too would get pulled into our meetings because we needed to understand some accounting issues or they had a question only a lawyer could answer. More contacts.

Another visit or two and all the receptionists and assistants knew me. If you think those people are beneath you or unimportant, think again. They are all potential allies in your quest to understand, and ingratiate yourself with, the client. It got to the point where they treated me as if I worked there. Equally important, they liked me because I liked them. I genuinely enjoyed getting to know them and letting them get to know me. Some of them are still friends. But it has to be sincere or you're wasting your time.

Consider the following: the receptionist controls access to the business. If you really need to get through to someone, voicemail ranks a distant second to having a receptionist or executive assistant track them down. When a key contact has a busy calendar that is closed to all, it's incredible that you can find your way in for a critical fifteen-minute meeting (that might change your life)—if the executive's assistant likes you! One of my clients used to travel with Krispy Kreme donuts for a particular assistant who had a weakness for them. He was always preparing for the moment when he'd have to ask a critical favour. But I digress.

The client visit is a critical strategy for many reasons. Consider also that every client has a choice of counsel. When you're first introduced, they see you only as the lawyer who is handling a single matter for them. Just another legal service provider. Maybe you are one of a handful of law firms they use.

The client visits over time allowed me to know each client's business from the inside, putting me a step ahead of the pack. I learned their challenges because I was experiencing the clients' reactions to problems and crises in real time at their place of work. I built a critical understanding of the internal dynamics of their decision-making team. In most cases my relationship began with the finance team and slowly migrated over to the C-suite. In one case I became an advisor to the CEO, competing with a board member, a senior partner at one of Canada's most prestigious law firms. Over time, I may not have displaced the other firms, but my share of client work grew.

You have a choice. Do you want to limit your relationship with the client to a call you receive, summarizing the problem as she perceives it? Her Perality. A call that could just as easily be made to one of your competitors? Instead you could be present regularly on the client premises, where you can learn the personalities and observe the internal politics, all critical to framing the solutions your clients are seeking. You also increase the probability that you will be on site as the problem emerges and before they can reach for the phone to call anyone else.

COVID-19 lessons for the future

In the current pandemic environment, client visits in many cases seem neither appropriate nor feasible. However, that assumption is correct only by conventional standards.

Time to step forward with some simple yet effective tactics to get in front of existing clients. Set up Zoom meetings between you and the client contacts. Offer a free seminar on an issue of interest or a new development. Encourage the client to line up a number of his or her contacts to attend. If your clients are in-house, figure out how to present information to qualify for continuing education credits. The key is to maintain a presence, getting your face in front of theirs in as many different creative ways as possible.

Most organizations are feeling similar challenges: personnel working from home, with a resulting loss of cohesion as well as a strain on corporate values—the same phenomena you may be experiencing in your own workplace. Employees, and in particular teams, are drifting apart. The isolation of physical distancing is not easily overcome.

Capitalize on that insecurity and work to improve the cohesion of your clients by bringing them together with regular seminars. The areas do not have to be your exclusive expertise. If you want to get creative, approach other subject-experts to speak to clients with you as moderator. The key is to keep contact. To stay in touch. To show you care.

Develop expertise

If your client sees you only as the person to call when they have a particular problem that's festering, you're cheating yourself of the possibility of a rich experience. You will look indistinguishable to them from all the other forgettable/interchangeable professionals they deal with daily. How do you make yourself stand out?

There will be little interest in you if you can't identify your expertise and distinguish yourself from the bunch. I learned that early in my career from Nash, one of my high school buddies, at a networking event. After the obligatory schmooze, Nash asked if I could do a shareholder agreement for his family business.

"Our law firm told me they can do it for thirty-five hundred dollars. Could you do it for less?"

I knew enough about shareholder agreements to know that to do it properly I needed to invest time and effort. And family situations are rife with potential problems and conflict around succession that need to be fully discussed before they are papered.

I told him I couldn't do it. I wanted to be a lawyer who is regarded for expertise, not for being the cheapest alternative. That's just a race to the bottom. As in any business, there will always be someone out there prepared to undercut you on price. The clients who are only interested in the bargain will never respect you. Ultimately, they will leave you. That's not to say you can't succeed delivering better pricing. More about that below.

Here are some examples of ways to distinguish yourself:

1. If you're drawn to technology, master it.

Faster, cheaper, better: three words that have been driving commercial innovation for the last century. In the beginning there was Ford and the Model T. Flash forward to the reshaping of the distribution of goods through big box stores and more recently through online delivery systems. Walmart, Amazon, Microsoft, Facebook, Apple, Uber, Peloton, Tesla: just a few of the names that are challenging every paradigm from bricks and mortar stores to the way we eat, sleep, exercise and work. All built on technology.

Does technological proficiency apply to professional service? How can it not? Has the legal profession adjusted? Not nearly as rapidly as it ought. Until recently, the professions—and particularly lawyers—have been pretending these rules do not apply to them in the same way.[45]

While many massive corporations rely on service suppliers who can deliver volume work cheaply and efficiently, major professional service firms are providing high-value services at massive premiums

---

45. The thought leaders in technological innovation and its impact on the future of professional service are Richard Susskind and Mark Cohen. For their views on a post-COVID world, tune in to this debate. https://bit.ly/3iWrWRR

without complaint from these clients. Those professional firms, however, represent a tiny fragment of the professional service market. Almost everyone else in the profession is learning to adapt. One large firm has appointed a lawyer in his sixties to run their innovation program. Doesn't that sound like a contradiction in terms? (Though it could work if the team beneath him were young and enthusiastic.) Some firms might be better off hiring college students.

A number of young professional entrepreneurs have discovered how to use technical innovation to deliver lower-cost service. For example, one firm of mortgage enforcement lawyers figured out how to cut the unnecessary time and overhead out of repetitive process: faster, more efficient, cheaper.

Years ago, one US firm separated from the pack by doing what was then unthinkable for professionals but so obvious to manufacturing companies. They broke their litigation files down into tiny compartmentalized processes, like an auto manufacturing plant. Then they formed a team for each process to figure out if it was necessary, and if so, how to reduce time spent performing the service. Their novel concept was not about delivering the most thoughtful service. It was about delivering the best result at the lowest price point. Institutions flocked to them like pigeons to bread crumbs. They weren't smarter than the rest of us—just more innovative.

If you want to compete in this area, it can be highly lucrative. Technology can drive down costs by allowing you to minimize lawyer time on a bulk of files and replace it with clerk time or software. The work may be crushingly mundane for a lawyer, but software doesn't care what it's doing. Just ask Alexa!

Mastery of technology that will simplify your clients' lives can distinguish you. Once you have that expertise, you can sell it by focusing on the clients who can buy it. "Faster, more efficient, cheaper" may suit you better than more sophisticated, expensive work that you may not yet have the contacts to generate.

A word of caution. Do not for a moment believe that underbidding for repetitive work where you have developed a niche will allow you access to the institution's more lucrative work. In my experience it rarely, if ever, works that way. One major firm set up an incredible system for mortgage enforcement for banks in a tiny office outside Toronto. The concept was pure genius and profitable. But it led to none of the banks' high-end lucrative work. My own firm was renowned for its management-side employment expertise. You would think we could translate that to the clients' commercial work. It rarely happened.

You will become known for your niche, but a firm that hires you because you provide superb service for a specific need at a low price is unlikely to hire you for anything complicated of high value. You need to decide where you want to be in the value chain. You might have an incredibly successful career generating low-cost work at high margins—as long as that's what you want.

2. Learn the lingo of your clients' industry

Learning about your client and their business requires you to speak their language. Just as lawyers have their "whereas"s, "notwithstanding"s, and "quid pro quo"s, accountants have their "widgets" and countless other professional bits of jargon that they take for granted when speaking to one another. So does every other industry, as do most companies. Learning the difference between "above the line" and "below the line" was among my first lessons when dealing with film producers—the first of hundreds of similar terms of art learned by sweat equity. Over time it will become obvious what phrases are part of everyday usage and are important for your development. Once you can speak the language of a client's industry, you open doors to develop other work within that industry.

3. Get involved with a particular industry

Pick one that interests you. All you need is one client with a niche to begin. The starting point is to figure out the connection between your client, its problem, and others experiencing similar issues.

Go to the events tied to that business sector. That's where your clients will be. That's where your clients will introduce you to others in their industry and speak well of you. Volunteer your time with those organizations. Offer to write. Offer to speak. Offer to join committees that you may eventually lead. That is time well invested in yourself.

Hugo Alves, the CEO of Auxly, a cannabis company, has done this not just once, but twice in his career. His story is a case study further on, but the time he invested in learning about all the potential sub-industries in cannabis, before it was legalized, propelled his career from lawyer to entrepreneur.

4. If you build it, they will come

This advice is the toughest advice to follow, because the client you want may take you years to connect with and years to attract. Most times the door will open, not when you plan to open it, but when it happens on its own. At that moment you have to be prepared to kick it in!

I was in my fifth year in practice when I stepped up and made the decision to hyper-focus on the entertainment industry. I wrote papers that were published in tax journals, and then I took excerpts to republish in industry periodicals. I attended conferences; I volunteered for industry committees; I came up with an idea I thought might appeal to every film and TV company in Canada and then slowly began meeting them. I found a few files with small producers and learned how to apply my theory in practice.

Two years later I got lucky. I met *one* client who would change the entire course of my career, and all the time I had invested in building and selling my expertise was put to use.

Where would I be today if I had not gotten out from behind my desk, if I had not taken the radical decision to risk stability of a house in the suburbs and three kids (with a fourth on the way) in Montreal and move the whole caravan to Toronto at the beginning of a world recession, all to open a tiny law office in Toronto—all this before my thirty-third birthday?

I arrived in a new market with a few connections. But I seized the moment, and by taking the kind of risks that became part of my DNA, in two short years I had transformed from a lawyer indistinguishable from the rest to an emerging expert in a particular industry that was itself on the rise.

Many of the ideas that I popularized in the entertainment industry were borrowed from others. That's not just me. That's business. There is often no great advantage to being the "first mover" into an area. The greatest successes in business were the innovators who improved what was already there. (You don't have to look further than Microsoft and Apple, among the world's most valuable companies.) I based my first few deals on ideas developed in California, and the most lucrative end of my tax practice was based on ideas conceived by a lawyer out in BC— aka the competition.[46]

> *You don't have to be a first mover. Take the ideas of others, improve them, master them, make them yours, and run with them.*

My career evolved by studying newly emerging trends, and if I saw some promise, I would take them and add my own twists. I started with a modest practice in July 1989 when I arrived in Toronto on the first day of a global recession. Within eight years I emerged as one of the leading tax lawyers in entertainment law in the world. My practice had grown by 4,000 percent. I didn't have to reinvent the wheel to get there. I just remodelled it a little and grew with my most aggressive clients.[47]

If you see something trending that interests you, jump on it. You do have to give luck the chance to present itself. You begin by

46. He finally gets a shout-out. Thank you, Rob Strother.

47. In my next book, *Triple F*, you'll read the story of the rise of Walied Soliman, who used a combination of ingenuity and fearlessness to build a remarkable career in the lucrative field of hostile takeovers.

strengthening your basic legal skills. While doing so, you distinguish yourself by writing and speaking on the expertise you are developing. There are hundreds of outlets to publish on your own or to post your work online. Maybe no one is noticing? You might wonder.

You need only one person to notice. One prospect, one mentor, is all it takes One person who needs what you have to offer because you stand out. Then you build it out from there. It's your investment in yourself.

5. Take a basic accounting course

At some point in your practice you are going to need to know how to interpret information on a balance sheet or an income statement. It's near impossible to go through a career in law without being able to decipher these. Many of us turned to law because we were afraid of numbers, but if you can push through that fear, you'll find that basic financial literacy is a huge boost, regardless of whether you're in private practice, in-house, or doing business, family law, or litigation. At some point the dreaded balance sheet is going to cross your path.

I find debits and credits boring as all hell, but understanding what goodwill means or the difference between short-term and long-term debt, or how you calculate inventory, is kind of basic. Whether your client is evaluating a business acquisition, handling a piece of commercial litigation, or dividing up matrimonial assets, a knowledge of basic accounting will allow you to ask more effective questions of accounting experts. The more informed you are, the less the client will see you as *only* the legal advisor and the more likely you are to become a trusted business advisor. A critical transformation.

There's a secondary benefit to understanding some basic accounting. Whether you stick around and become a partner in a law firm, move in-house, or use your law degree for any other business purpose, your financial literacy is critical. The litigator who needs to cross-examine an accountant to find out where the assets are hidden must be able to ask informed questions. A family law practitioner needs to understand how assets are being divided in a separation or divorce. That necessitates being able to decipher the opposing party's financial information.

Working Smarter

If your career is successful, you will spend considerable time learning from your research, from others, and from falling flat on your face, before finally mastering new situations. Is success reserved for those who outwork you—or are there more important factors that go into building your career?

Ryan Middleton used to be the hardest working associate I ever met. He figured he could outwork everyone to build his client base. Things were progressing much more slowly than he anticipated, he wasn't spending enough time with family, and he was developing a reputation as a "service guy."

Today he's a partner at Dentons Canada LLP, a part of the world's largest firm. When I interviewed him, I asked whether his advance was the product of a nose-to-grindstone approach. It turns out it was exactly the opposite. Ryan had a turning-point moment that set him off in a new direction. "Originally I determined that I just had to work harder than anyone else to get ahead. Except all that was getting me was a pat on the back. ***Things changed when I finally became strategic.***"

Ryan finally figured out what I had learned. I was getting the work because I was there before the client knew they had a problem. I was working on the solution three weeks before they would have called anyone else to discuss it. Ryan nailed it with the following conclusion, which he wants to pass on to you: ***"I spent more time listening and less time advising."***

Exactly the opposite of what you might expect.

"Over time I learned how their business worked. What drove their internal decision-making. I understood the economics behind the decision-making. In short, I had integrated myself into the business."

Ryan also learned a valuable lesson that he put to work: "Most clients' problems are tied to particulars of their business. If they don't have to spend two hours indoctrinating you about the business unit just so you can understand the question, you're saving them an enormous amount of time."

Ryan expresses the value of the learning from the service provider's perspective. TVO's Mark Le Blanc makes the same point from the other side. "I can't afford to spend time educating my outside counsel on how my business operates when I have a problem. It's something I expect them to have learned."

When faced with the choice, who is the general counsel more likely to call for advice, the advisor who understands the business or the one who does not?

Sometimes I would meet a client, or a contact at an industry event who was being served by another firm, and we would share experiences about an issue of interest to them. A few months later I might be reading a trade or legal journal that twigged to the issue we had been discussing. I would clip out the article, circle the key paragraphs in red marker, and send it off to the client or contact. I wanted them to believe I was spending my entire life thinking about their business.

At one point or another my firm represented almost every significant film and television production company in eastern Canada. They were competitors with one another, but we had them all convinced that I was the only tax lawyer in the business with a finger on the pulse of everything going on in their industry and in their particular business.

To be valuable, you need to understand more than the law. If you want to make rain repeatedly, I recommend you learn the business end of your client's industry—and you do that by being there! Remember one final point:

The easiest way to grow your practice is to help your clients grow.

Marketing–Networking–Mentorship–Sponsorship

How do we market ourselves?

How do I get my name out there? How do I expand my network? These are questions you should always think about. The problem is that there is a never-ending assortment of events to choose from: cocktail parties, bar association events, charities, young professional networking, mornings, lunches, evenings—it never ends. How much of it is a complete waste of my precious time? How do I fit marketing into my schedule, when I'm completely overloaded in the office? How do I deal with the discomfort of milling around with a group of strangers? Here are three pieces of advice to help you get started.

Prioritize your time

Your most precious commodity is your time. Be strategic. Make tough choices. For every event you might attend, first ask yourself, why? Are you going to meet clients? If it's a bar association event, are you going to learn something important? Have you seen enough of family or friends lately? If you must attend an event, do you have to be there for the entire event? If not, do what you have to do—then leave.

Over the years I devised a strategy for cocktail/dinner and award events that I attended, particularly with a young family waiting at home. My goal was to touch base with no more than three key people. I went, I met, I chatted, I left. I called it "working the room," but it was a "room" of my creation: no more than the few key people I needed to see. The conversation had to be more than social. I came prepared with business questions or conversation ideas that would give me an excuse to follow up later.

Many nights I set time limits. Sometimes it was thirty minutes, sometimes an hour. Rarely four hours to sit through a dinner. Things might have been different if I'd been single and it was a social occasion. I got what I needed—an excuse to follow up over the next week with the person I'd met.

There is no universal rule. Other times I went to a dinner but only because there was a chance I might get an hour or two with a key contact. In those cases, I made certain to sit beside the target. Sitting at a dinner with a group of strangers or "filling a table" by agreeing to take a seat will not advance your career. However, if your work-team leader calls on you to fill that seat, you must weigh your role on the team against the implications of refusing. No one ever said the choices would be easy. But when possible, choose your seat strategically. Use the evening as a chance to converse with someone you need to get to know better.

Before every event decide whom you want to meet and speak to. Set that as your goal. Once you've achieved the goal, you can leave. As we'll discuss later, collecting business cards at events is not a strategy. Leaving *one person* you met with a lasting impression is a far better tactic. Devise your own strategy that fits your strengths, your goals, and your vision. Tailor the playbook.

Maryse Bertrand, the successful Montreal corporate lawyer, put it succinctly: ***"Decide what counts for you, then prioritize your life accordingly."***

Ask for favours: the Ben Franklin effect

Networking is so much more than going out in public and meeting strangers. Not only is that hard work, but it's tough, inefficient marketing. Here's a secret a number of us have learned through experience. Sometimes the best form of networking is seeking advice.

I asked TVO's Mark Le Blanc about his secret to building a network. His reply: "Find someone more senior whom you respect and ask them for advice. Go for coffee or lunch. Don't be shy to ask."

I have to confess that some of the best career advice I received came from people who had no idea they were giving it. I never forgot their kindness and kept in touch with most of them along the course of my career.

We tend to assume that in order to ingratiate ourselves with others, we need to do them favours. Asking for help is usually the last thing we think of doing. Some instinct in us mistakenly makes us believe that asking a favour is a sign of weakness. The reverse is often true. It is far easier to strike up a relationship with someone who agrees to do a favour for you.

This advice ties back to a Ben Franklin anecdote.[48] For years he had difficulty with a political opponent and finally had the idea of asking the opponent to lend him a rare first edition book. Here is the excerpt from his memoirs:

Having heard that he had in his library a certain very scarce and curious book, I wrote a note to him, expressing my desire of perusing that book, and requesting he would do me the favour of lending it to me for a few days. He sent it immediately, and I return'd it in about a week with another note, expressing strongly my sense of the favour. When we next met in the House, he spoke to me (which he had never done before), and with great civility; and he ever after manifested a readiness to serve me on all occasions, so that we became great friends, and our friendship continued to his death.

The fellow was so proud to be able to provide the book to his nemesis, Franklin, that the ice was broken. From that moment forward they forged a relationship. Some psychologists speculate that once you have agreed to do the favour, some part of your brain convinces you that the beneficiary must be nicer than you had been prepared to admit. How else can you justify doing something beneficial for them?

Putting aside the psychological evaluation of the roots, it seems that if you ask someone you would like to get to know for a favour, be it advice or an introduction to someone you need to meet to advance your career, you are far more likely to form a relationship with that person.

Whatever it is, do not be shy. The worst that can happen is that they will refuse, and the best is that a new door will open on your career path. Once again, overcome that fear of asking.

48. If you can make the time for Walter Isaacson's biography on *Benjamin Franklin, An American Life,* it is well worth the read.

Create relationships with mentors and sponsors

The Ben Franklin story is an appropriate lead-in to how you can benefit from others to advance your career. On your journey you will encounter two types of personalities who can help you get ahead, mentors and sponsors. They serve different purposes.

Mentors are those who monitor your progress and point you in the right direction. They are the people you go to with questions, or who decide to give you advice. Sometimes it's advice you want to hear, and other times it's criticism about how you've performed. The latter is much tougher medicine to swallow. Once you pick yourself up off the floor, your ability to bounce back, learn, and advance will leave you far further ahead of where you'd be after a pat on the back, which momentarily feels good but, most of the time, isn't going to leave you with a lasting lesson.

Many firms attach mentors to young professionals. Not all mentors have the skills, patience, inclination, or experience to help. If you're in a situation like that, reach out to others in the firm with whom you work. The more mentors you have, the better. I recommend you find the toughest professionals or business people you can manage to deal with. They will teach you the most. In my case, two lawyers took me under their wings;[49] they drove me insane for the first five years of my career, but were critical in forming the solid foundation on which I built my practice.

Early on I learned two lessons from those mentors. The first: to perfect my thoughts in writing before expressing them in an argument. Oral discussion often glosses over points that cannot hide from criticism when reduced to writing. The second was tougher to learn. In situations where I was not certain how to resolve an issue, instead of presenting both sides without a conclusion as to the better view (for which I was repeatedly reamed), I was sent back to my office to stake out a position and defend it. It was okay to be wrong. It was not okay to waffle. That

---

49. Thank you, Daniel Levinson and Richard Lewin.

lesson served me enormously well in client meetings for my entire career. Clients want and need direction.

Hugo Alves, the Auxly CEO, points to the mentorship of Kip Daechsel, a senior lawyer in his firm, as being formative to his experience. One story stands out so many years later.

"I was young and wild in my first few years," Hugo admits. "Kip was helpful in reining me in and forcing me to understand the rigors and values that are key to professional success."

What did that mean in real terms? "I worked like a beast and my work was excellent, but the occasional Friday morning it was obvious that I'd been out the night before. He never chewed me out. He was far more subtle. 'You know,' Hugo, he said, 'no one will remember if you pulled an all-nighter at work, but they'll never trust you if you show up on a Friday like this. You need to let clients…you need to let *me* know that you won't let us down.'"

In one simple exchange Kip taught Hugo the lesson of Perality. Hugo also discovered, on his own, that if he arrived at meetings with written notes about the potential issues, he was beginning the meeting miles ahead of his peers. It got him noticed by clients and more senior lawyers. I wish I'd thought of that.

Mentors are to be distinguished from sponsors—the people who actively help you advance. In larger firms, no one gets to partnership without at least one politically savvy backer pushing their candidacy.

Both women and racially diverse professionals regularly speak of the critical importance of sponsors (often white men) to help them move ahead.

A client can also play the role of sponsor, talking you up to others, introducing and recommending you to new contacts, or upselling you within her organization. Sometimes a sponsor will introduce you to industry leaders or do you all kinds of other professional favours.

Jennifer Pollock, of Ratehub, puts it simply. "I've found success by keeping my network alive. Whenever I switched jobs, I made sure to give enough notice. I don't want to ever burn a bridge. I try to keep doors open and I value the relationships I've developed along the way. Sometimes it's coffee with a former colleague who was helpful, or a congratulatory email on their success. One of my old managers referred me for the position I'm in currently, so I know it works."

Sponsors can even play a critical role at the beginning of your career. Aaron Bains tells the story of his very tough articling year at Aird & Berlis. "I didn't shine that year, I was making mistakes, and initially I was not offered a hire-back position. Most students would have taken their foot off the pedal at that point. I did the opposite.

"One of the senior lawyers in the firm was in need of a student for his financing transactions. His associate at the time brought me in to help. Tony had a reputation for demanding and expecting excellence. Our first meeting was supposed to be 'sometime' on Friday. We were finally able to sit down at 7:30 pm. In my mind, I should have been out drinking with my colleagues. Instead I was doing a slow burn. He reviewed the first memo I delivered, pointing out some errors, but he also made sure to praise what I had done well. He offered me a drink from his "office bar." We sat and talked for a few hours, by which time he owned me. No one had ever taken that much interest in me. And I was not even being hired back!

"For the last few months I worked my tail off for Tony on a huge debt finance transaction. In the midst of all this, his associate left private practice, leaving just me. Tony came up with a plan to build up the number of sponsors that would support asking management to change their minds and hire me back as a lawyer. I had to execute the plan, but I'm sure Tony was working behind the scenes as well. Five years later I am doing what I love, climbing the ladder at the firm."

Can you do it on your own? Perhaps. But experience shows that, like Aaron, you are far more likely to succeed with the help of people with credibility.

This applies equally to seeking new clients. As you'll see later, you're more likely to be retained by someone who has heard good things about you than by making cold calls. As a rule of thumb, it takes seven encounters with a prospect to convert them to a client. (This *rule of sevens* is a subject of my next book on advanced skills.) A sponsor can shorten the delay between meeting a new contact and convincing them to send you work.

Do not leave this chapter without listening to the valuable
information in this podcast on networking:
Talkabouttalk.com/45-networking

Jennifer Lee tells me some of her most important leadership lessons came from more senior partners at Deloitte.

"One in particular told me that as I was progressing, I had to be much more conscious of what I said to younger professionals. 'People are paying attention to every word,' he reminded me. I never really thought of myself as a role model. Even now with my global position, I still have trouble seeing it. But I know I have a duty to set an example. My words matter. My actions matter. People are watching. I understand that my mentor's most important advice, though he never expressed it this way, was 'be a mentor.' That has instilled in me a deep desire—I'd call it a duty—to pay it forward."

Case studies

Tara Vasdani

In 2019, Tara, a second-year lawyer, was ready to open up her own shop.[50] She had a few client leads—not much more. She also needed a business name. Since she'd been writing about remote work and artificial intelligence for about a year, she went with Remote Law Canada. A quick, instinctive choice, but a prescient decision.

Once she had the name, she continued to expand her knowledge about remote work, to write about it, and to reach out to others in the field. Eventually a reporter noticed her, and a story about Tara's practice was published in *Forbes* online. The article led to some offers to speak. Did Tara know more about work-from-home issues than the thousands of employment lawyers in the country, most of them far more advanced in their careers? Probably not. But she had the name, and because of all her marketing, she was developing a reputation.

---

50. This is the same Tara from the Introduction.

Creating a perception for others that she had the expertise. The Perality is that most clients do not need the foremost expert. Especially for routine matters. They want an expert who is top of mind.

Tara opened her firm at a moment in time when small, low-overhead remote companies were beginning to pop up all over the country, some as small boutiques, others in larger federations. But her marketing and initiative put her on the consideration list for *Canadian Lawyer*'s Top 25 Most Influential Lawyers in 2018 and 2019 as a "Young Influencer and Changemaker," and in 2020 again, for her focus on remote work.

Shortly afterward a pandemic shut down the entire world, and she found herself a world expert on a subject that was the bull's eye of international attention. Right place. Right time. Was it luck? She'd gravitated to a subject matter that interested her, one that fit with her own practice. She marketed the heck out of it. Then the lightning struck. Instead of falling over like the rest of us, Tara captured it in a bottle.

Hugo Alves

Hugo knew little about cannabis law before it was legalized,[51] but he had learned plenty about being on the front end of a wave from his days as a young associate at Bennett Jones. When he'd joined the firm years earlier, he floundered for a while before being taken under the wing of Gray Taylor, a partner who desperately needed an associate to help with fourteen opinions on an environmental financing deal. Hugo knew nothing about the area. As it turns out, he was not alone. It was shortly after the Kyoto Protocols, which meant nothing to him. As he puts it, "Everything I learned on that deal was breaking new ground. There were no precedents, so we had to beg, borrow, and steal from other types of financing deals. This was the wild west of emission financings."

One deal led to the next until Gray and Hugo were known as the *world leaders* in the field. "But not without fourteen-hour drafting

---

51. Law schools were examining the constitutional basis for the legalization of cannabis for medicinal purposes. Students might have been experiencing first-hand the impact of unlawful cannabis consumption on professional school grades.

sessions, three-thousand-hour years, hyper-focus on a single client, billions of dollars of transactions. By 2013 the entire sector was dead. All that expertise was worth zero." That is a story that may cause many of you to cringe. I doubt I could have worked that hard or sacrificed that much for a great associate review, a pat on the back, and a bonus. The crux of the life lesson arrived a few years later.

"Emission trading was dead, but the buzz about cannabis—no pun intended—was beginning. None of the big firms or the institutions would go anywhere near it in those days before legalization, but it looked like an opportunity. I decided to take a risk and learn it. Once again there were no precedents, no rules or regulations, just a lot of maybes. But I had a dream. When the world thought about cannabis, I wanted them to think Hugo Alves.

"I began to write articles, offered to speak at industry conferences, then began to invest the time putting the conferences together, then chairing them. It was all volunteer work. Speaking, writing, introducing myself to everyone at all levels of the emerging culture. No one had financing, no one had money, no one could do anything legally, except for medicinal. None of this was billable, so it became my full-time job on top of the other full-time job at the firm, where I docketed hours and got paid for that. By the time the industry was legalized, I knew everyone, I was respected as the Canadian expert, and I was years ahead of the competition."

What caused Hugo to move from Bennett Jones into a leading role as an entrepreneur is a story for another chapter.

Applying this advice to your career

Every year new areas of law are developing. Currently the world is focused on the large aging population, artificial intelligence (which is shorthand for countless new technologies), internet and financial service security, emerging crypto currencies, climate change, water rights issues, Indigenous rights, the #MeToo movement, driverless cars, and drones and robotics, pandemics and employment law, just to name a few. Every new development generates unique legal issues that you can master as well as anyone in the world, because the issues are unique and untested.

> *When it comes to evolving issues, the playing field is level.*
> *Any one of us can emerge as the leader.*

What about the future? Casting our gaze five years forward, industries that we cannot imagine today will exist. From a professional perspective the emerging areas for mastery are countless and favour tech-savvy, supple-minded, ambitious young professionals whose brains are not mired in how things used to work. Are you willing to invest and take a chance on yourself, like Hugo Alves and Tara Vasdani?

> *The key skill of the future is adaptability.*

Charting this chapter

Rather than looking at practice building as if it were a linear progression, it may be easier to understand as a cycle that looks something like this:

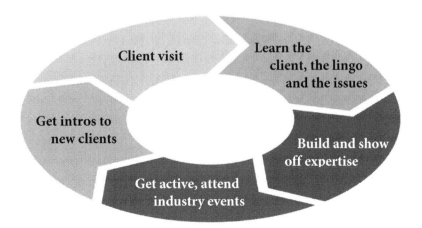

Each of these activities needs to be going on simultaneously. As you saw from the case studies above, as early as your second year of practice you can be working toward all of these goals.

Don't be bound by convention

This chapter concludes with a remarkable story of success, told by a man who came to Canada as a teenager with nothing but the shirt on his back. A man who went on to build a most remarkable career in shareholder services by turning every conventional approach on its ear. A man who is leading the movement toward increased diversity in Canadian business.

When I first met Wes Hall (who appears in Chapter 10) over fifteen years ago, I was surprised at his youth. He was the CEO of Kingsdale Shareholder Services—now Kingsdale Advisors—a company successfully competing with major trust companies in shareholder relations. I asked him how he achieved so much success so early in his career.

"Rather than start my business at the bottom and struggle to find small companies who needed services to manage their shareholder communication, I decided to take the opposite approach. I came up with a concept that I thought would work at any level and then tried to sell it to the largest elephants. I concluded that if I could sell just one of them on what I was building, I could figure out the rest and scale down, rather than scale up. I put every ounce of energy into creating that platform and I projected confidence in my approach and design.

"I met with Sun Life just after they demutualized. They had over three million shareholders. They liked what I had to offer. Right time and right place. From that point it was all downhill."

I kicked myself after that meeting with Wes. Why had I not ever thought of that? Most of us simply assume that as unknowns, we will never get the attention of key decision makers. We've been taught to think small to start, prove ourselves, build on our successes, build upon them, pay our dues, wait our turn.

If you have the gumption and the guts, there is another way. It's unconventional, but Wes is a living example that if you live your career like you have nothing to lose, you have so much to gain.

In the next chapter we take a look inside the beast. I'm not referring to Wes—it's something much bigger.

CHAPTER 12

How Do Professional Service Firms Work?

Whether you intend to go into practice for yourself or to join a firm, you need to understand the business basics of the profession.

From twenty-five years of leadership experience, I know law firms inside out. They run like other professional service firms—all fairly straightforward businesses. In that sense they are not much different than the ice cream parlour that makes its own varieties of gelato.

Take the case of my fictional aunt Queenie. She injected capital and borrowed from the bank to rent a storefront, buy her ingredients, and purchase the expensive machinery to churn her homemade secret recipes into cups and cones that she sells to families six days a week. Queenie had fixed targets on sales necessary to keep her afloat. The first three thousand cones each week paid the overhead, including the wages of the college students who served the customers. Her goal is to manufacture, fill the buckets, and get them scooped out the door and paid for quickly. If her ice cream sits in the freezer for days and weeks, she'll go out of business. Simple.

Instead of cups and cones, the professional firm inventory consists of the hours worked by the professionals that have to be entered into a computer system, billed, and collected. (We'll discuss more inventive business models further on.)

Unlike the machine that sits on Queenie's floor in the back room and churns the air into the cream, freezes the mixture, and pours it into containers, the professional machine stands on two legs, leaves the office (or logs out) every night, and returns (or logs in) the next morning. Taking lawyers as an example, I can tell you they are expensive. Every year they expect raises that outpace inflation. They take up space that has to be rented, and they use resources, like assistants, to manage their countless tasks. In larger firms, librarians help guide the research and order the right services, and marketing experts help secure new clients and establish the brand. Keeping up with advances in technology is also expensive.

All of these expenses are financed by a combination of capital from partners, bank debt, and cash flow from operations. If you imagine your hour of work as a container of gelato, the longer that hour sits in the freezer, unpaid for, the more the firm has to borrow or inject more capital to cover the expenses. The professional's goal is to enter that hour in the billing system, bill it, and collect it from the client as quickly as possible. This metric is called "turnover," and firm managers refer to it in evaluating professionals. Managing that turnover time is the essence of practice management. Putting it really simply, there is a huge focus on the billable hour (which gets its own chapter later), the need to docket time promptly, and the importance of collecting your bills quickly.

The business model for professional service

If you're in the business of selling hours of inventory, your revenue is limited. A day has only twenty-four hours,[52] of which a third (should) go to sleep. If you arrive at nine in the morning and work until six, subtracting an hour for lunch, that leaves eight hours available for work that can be sold to customers. With coffee breaks and so on, if you can get seven chargeable hours out of the eight, you are doing well. Multiply that by fifty weeks a year (allowing for two weeks of vacation) and you're delivering 1,750 hours. That is respectable for an associate.

---

52. I do know one famous lawyer eventually reprimanded by his firm for docketing over twenty-four hours in a day. He did have an excuse. He spent his life on cross-continent flights, reviewing documents between meetings. With the seven-hour time difference returning home and no sleep, he recorded a thirty-hour day.

Here's a rule of thumb that applies to most firms. In the legal industry it's known as the rule of thirds. You need to docket and collect at least three times your salary to be profitable for your firm. One third goes to overhead, one third goes into your bank account as salary, and the final third is the bottom line shared by the partners (the owners of the business), who do not earn a salary. Without your one-third contribution, the firm cannot survive.

For partners the math is a little different, since they are not earning a salary. Instead they share the profits, to which you are contributing with your one third.[53]

Let's look at those 1,750 hours and assume that your billing rate is $300 per hour. This means you are worth $525,000, assuming the firm bills and collects every last dollar. If you are earning $175,000, you are at the equilibrium point.

If you happen to be working on a large ongoing file, it's easy to make those seven hours a day. If you're a junior securities law associate working on an investment banking deal, you're probably doing ten to twelve hours a day, and if you have to pull an all-nighter, even better for the firm. All the client cares about is closing quickly. Don't expect to sleep much or see your friends while that's happening, but the head of your department is going to be very happy.

The news is not nearly as good if, like most practitioners, you have five to ten files on your desk, with clients calling all day long, requiring you to open and close various files. You will discover that if that turns into five hours billed, it's a lot. That ends up closer to 1,250 hours. At $300 per hour that translates to $375,000. While there is enough money to pay you and your overhead ($350,000 in total), the partners are making about $25,000 on you. If they have to write off even 5 percent of your time (about $18,000), there is virtually nothing left for the partnership.

---

53. The partners are contributing economically with all their personal billed and collected time, less their individual share of the overhead attributable to them. That math is never easy to justify and occasionally leads to fights among partners. This sometimes explains why some partners refuse to delegate work to younger associates (in order to improve their personal statistics and to appear more profitable to the leaders, who are allocating the partnership profits).

Remember, in harsh terms you are no more than the machine that generates the inventory of hours, but your machine is making the business no money. Unless your expertise is so important that the business can afford you as a loss leader, what do you think happens next? Eventually the head of associates will knock on your door to let you know your future prospects are limited. It may mean a salary cut, but more likely you should be considering your options.

Dealing with targets

What about the time you need to spend keeping up with new developments in the profession? Or the time that will go to training neophytes beneath you as you advance in your practice? The papers you will need to write to show off your expertise in particular areas? The speeches and presentations you will prepare to advance your other skills? Pro bono files that the firm will be encouraging you to take on?

Consider the large institutional clients who have negotiated bulk discount deals with your firm. They are both a blessing and a curse. A blessing in that the firm can count on these clients for huge chunks of the work done by the firm over the course of the year. They represent money in the bank, and a guarantee that the associates will not be twiddling their thumbs if the transactional work slows down, or if a phenomenon like coronavirus wipes out your transportation, restaurant, and hospitality clients. They are also a curse, in that the cost of the relationship is that the institution negotiates a considerable discount, perhaps 10 to 20 percent, off the firm's best rates.

If you're assigned to these types of files, your work becomes even less profitable—unless you make it up with more hours. Simple math shows that at a 10 percent discount to your hourly rate of $300, you only become profitable at about 1,900 hours billed and collected. If you are in that situation, you have to wonder whether the partners consider you a worthwhile investment. Are you developing broader skills and expertise that will result in future value, beyond the immediate "bottom-line" calculation? Welcome to the big leagues!

Suffice it to say, this is life in private practice. Firms have to balance between more profitable and less profitable clients. They need to keep you busy, and each firm has carved out its own niche and client base that allows them to continue operating.

The black swan

In recent years more nimble firms have begun looking for ways to reduce overhead. If you look at the office setup for firms like Deloitte in Toronto, you will see modern open-concept floors where workers operate in cubicles surrounded by natural light, while internal offices are set up as meeting or private think spaces. The old notion of the office for most employees has disappeared, drastically cutting the rent per professional.

In many firms, office sizes are shrinking, and in some cases, employees are being encouraged to work remotely from home. This saves precious commuting hours and reduces the rent (depending on how long the lease has to run). However, it also challenges the notion of collegiality as the essence of the professional firm experience. Can collegiality translate in Zoom meetings? The world is still finding out as I write these words.

The COVID-19 epidemic has caused the entire North American legal industry to rethink the viability and efficiency of remote work from home. Technology has advanced at breakneck pace to deal with confidentiality and the safety of home computer hookups. We have yet to see whether the quantum shift caused by the epidemic will change the way professional firms look at the high cost of office space, the time wasted by a commuting workforce, and the flexibility of work-at-home alternatives as an ongoing trend. Weighing against those considerations is the drop in collegiality, or the social glue, that holds people and organizations together. The issues are complex to navigate.

What is the partnership track and why should you care?

The partnership question is generally misunderstood by most young professionals and particularly lawyers. Sadly, that misunderstanding can carry them through their seventh, eighth, or ninth year of practice, long beyond the point when they should have known (or at least sought out) the answer.

If you want to take charge of where you are heading, it's a question you will ask and keep asking throughout your progression. Many firms don't really address the issue of partnership head on. They assume you will figure it out for yourself.

Even at my old firm, Heenan Blaikie, some of the departments were more open about what they expected in terms of development than others. My personal test was simple.

Partnership is recognition that you are acting like an owner of my business. I would take associates to lunch and explain to them what that meant to me. They needed to demonstrate independence from the more senior people who had been feeding them their work. They needed a simple but effective plan of goals they wanted to achieve over the coming year. They needed to show me they were prepared to continue to grow. In my firm, built on the premise that everyone needed to contribute to the bottom line, they had to understand how they were going to do that. Often I knew within a month of a lawyer joining the firm whether they had the potential. Those were the people we invested in. We didn't want them to leave! Those were the people we brainwashed to stay.

If you're thinking partnership is this mysterious one-way street, think again. There are two lanes on this road: yours and the firm's. They may never meet. You may be putting in the time until the next career move presents itself. The firm may be thinking the exact same thing, waiting for you to leave. In the more advanced businesses, they will assist you with the outplacement.

The major accounting firms have programs to build the skill sets of potential partners. They readily admit they stream candidates. If you're not in the stream you desire, start thinking about career alternatives. Don't wait.

If you've managed to latch on to the right sponsors, they will give you a rundown of what you need to understand about partnership at the place you're at, and they will sell you on why you need to stay and what you need to do to get there. That represents a very small percentage of all of you reading this book!

You still may not understand what I'm driving at in terms of becoming a partner. Let's go back to our ice cream parlor, where this chapter began. Imagine you've been a loyal employee, diligently serving customers for seven years. Would you have any expectation that the owner would give or sell to you a share in her business? You know the answer.

Would your answer be different if you had come up with the idea for four new flavours and as a result, sales tripled? Or if people showed up to hear you sing opera every afternoon and you could point at sales in that period doubling? If you created the technology to move the ice cream inventory out the door much faster to improve the bottom line? Or if you volunteered to develop a plan to franchise the business?

The faithful employee who is not adding to the business should never expect to become a part owner of the business. Yet hundreds and thousands of North American young professionals don't ever try to translate that notion to their own work.

Your fiscal literacy

A professional partnership is a business. The owners are entrepreneurs. When they admit new partners (usually by selling a small percentage of the ownership, referred to by many firms as "points"), they are selling them a share of the business. You go from employee to owner. But are you prepared for that moment? Have you learned anything about the finances of the business you are buying? Have you ever seen its balance sheet? Do you know anything of its annual revenues, how they are divided between divisions, what the margins are? The average credit line balance? How efficient the firm is with its work in progress? Can you even follow the jargon in this paragraph? Do you want to?

So many young professionals feel "so honoured" to be admitted to partnership that they do none of the due diligence. If you're planning to become an owner of a professional business, you need to understand how it works. You need to be financially literate. You need to do the diligence you would insist upon on behalf of a client. Even shareholders in public companies, who are completely uninvolved in management, often learn more about the businesses they are investing in than professionals know about the partnerships they aspire to join.

Why would a business want to admit as a partner someone who has done so little over a long period of time to understand the business? Many lawyers in big firms complain that there is no transparency, no road map, that the whole process is a complete secret. Do you want to stay in a firm like that? Yet so many lawyers muddle through the years, content to worry about their performance as lawyers, not bothering to learn anything about the business end of the law and failing to do the due diligence that they would readily undertake for clients. A shocking contrast.

As you will see in my next book, there is so much to learn in growing your own business skills. But if you have any aspirations to join a partnership, small or large, you need to develop the literacy to understand how the business works. How else can you decide whether it's a business worth joining, or even whether you want to join it? How else do you convince the partners that you can add something to the business? Don't you want to be thoroughly prepared for the most important upcoming decision of your career? For me the answer was, and is, a resounding yes.

When I was faced with that decision, I had already learned Heenan Blaikie's business strengths and weaknesses. We were a dominant firm in labour law with a regional scope. I brought a niche advantage in an industry that was beginning to grow. I could see what I added, and the firm had built a steadfast loyalty in me by standing by me back when I was still learning and at times having difficulty adjusting to new responsibilities. They had invested in me, and I had a vision of how I could invest in them.

I had a dream, shared by the chair of the firm, to expand the firm. I had partners who I knew would support that aspiration. I understood the balance sheet, and I would eventually set out to make the fixes to allow us to expand the firm from fifty to almost six hundred lawyers over the next twenty-five years.

Most young professionals no longer see partnership as the "brass ring." For those of you in that camp, you can stop reading this section now. Skip ahead. However, if you want to understand what you're walking away from, then it's worth learning some basic accounting, and/or speaking to the partners of the firm about the business. Ask questions: How much capital is invested by partners? What is the firm's policy on borrowing? How efficient are they at collecting receivables?

Did you know that in most partnerships 20 percent of the clients generate 80 percent of the revenues?[54] It was my experience as managing partner, legal consultants speak of it regularly, and while not exact, it's pretty darn close. Consider the implications. Four out of five clients are relatively small clients of the business, which is reliant on one out of five to survive. What does that say about the vulnerability of the business? How do the clients break down by industry? What is the vulnerability of the business to downturns in particular business sectors or to pandemics? So many questions—in fact, the same questions you would be analyzing with a client if they were looking at buying a business. These are the issues you'll eventually have to consider if you want to be on the partnership track.

There is one building block critical to professional-services profitability and to the way professional services are consumed, and that is the subject of the following chapter.

---

54. This is an offshoot of the Pareto Principle, a nineteenth-century postulation that in many instances, roughly 80 percent of events result from 20 percent of the causes. It began with some research showing that in Italy, 80 percent of the land was owned by 20 percent of the population. It has been applied to business in general. See Marshall, Perry, (October 9,2013), *The 80/20 Rule of Sales: How to Find Your Best Customers*. Entrepreneur.

CHAPTER 13

The Billable Hour

Heralded as *the* innovation of the second half of the twentieth century, the billable hour and its companion, the hourly rate, forced lawyers to keep track of their time. In the olden days, predating the Cold War, lawyers would charge clients for the value of the work performed. Eventually an American figured out that if he charged by the hour, he would make a lot more money. That decision transformed private practice in America into big business.

For the non-elite firms, though, the paradigm is beginning to wobble.

The argument against the billable hour is obvious. Imagine for a moment that you are a client. Your lawyer makes the most money by spending more hours working on a matter. You, on the other hand, expect the job to be done as efficiently as possible, which delivers the most value at the lowest cost. That is the way most other industries measure success. But not lawyers. Lawyer and client are at cross purposes when it comes to billing, and the client must trust the lawyer to act in their best interest.

And yet three generations of lawyers have been married to the notion of the billable hour. Bob Tarantino, an expert on the subject,[55] puts it succinctly: *"[I]t's the only pricing mechanism we've come up with that adequately functions at the intersection of two critical components of the lawyer/client relationship: trust and risk."*

55. Tarantino, Bob. (2020, July 16). *not dead yet—the billable hour at the intersection of trust and risk.* LinkedIn.

Where does the trust come in? If I can settle a matter with a half-hour phone call or with twenty weeks of research and planning followed by a phone call, which option will I take? Particularly if my call is going to create a value for the client one hundred to five hundred times greater than the time I invest? The example puts aside ethical considerations, but highlights the problem that clients' and lawyers' business interests are not necessarily aligned. In an era where trust in institutions is waning, this is a growing industry problem.

Law industry discussion about alternative billing models has been going on for years. One idea that has taken hold involves setting project fees, where the law firm either bids for work by the bundle or sets a fixed price for a job, much like an auto mechanic. Accounting firms have been operating this way for years with their standard work. It's quite a bit easier with repetitive work, like mortgages, standard loan or employment agreements, or enforcement actions, but a lot more difficult in unique practices where each case is subject to many variables that will affect the amount of time the firm invests.

I always looked at my firm like a mutual fund. Some areas were more profitable than others; some were steady and paid the rent; others were flashy but riskier propositions. Over time it all balanced out.

The problem is that most lawyers (especially those in their earlier years) are not very good at making or holding to budgets, with the exception of a few firms who have specialized in creating models to cost out work. Furthermore, so many lawyers believe they are adding value, when clients' perception is that the work is commoditized and too expensive. Perality at work.

Is there another way to deal with the problem? One option is a path few lawyers are comfortable pursuing: the notion of value billing. Value billing is something I started doing thirty years ago. I set up arrangements with a number of key clients so that when they succeeded, my firm would benefit. That meant charging them small amounts, and sometimes nothing at all, when transactions we worked on together failed to happen; and billing considerable amounts when the deals closed. We shared the risk—we shared the reward. That was our bargain with one another. Essentially, my firm made money when the client profited. Some days we lost out, but if you look back over a period of fifteen years, we probably collected more than five times what we would have earned if I had billed by the hour. Our clients never complained because they too profited from the success. They saw the bargain as fair and they trusted us.

So many professionals who provide value-added services are afraid of raising the topic with clients. Once again fear trumps good business sense. Even if clients decline to accept the value proposition, you've had a discussion that allows them to perceive you in a new and valuable way. A way that distinguishes you from their other advisors. A way that suggests you understand your value to them. Perality at work again.

Value billing

As a function of becoming a valuable lawyer, I believe you must begin to think about how to value your extraordinary service.

Value billing is predicated on the notion that if I, as a lawyer, can create value for my client, then our interests are aligned. I will not spend more time on the matter than absolutely needs to be spent. The client is not paying me for how long it takes me. They are paying me for a desired result. In some cases, it's a gradient of desired possible outcomes. In other words, the amount billed will depend on the outcome achieved. The more value I can help create or the greater the costs I can help avoid, the higher the bill and vice versa.

The risk, of course, is that if the outcome is not the one either the lawyer or the client desires, I may spend considerable time to no end. But really, should I be paid if I've achieved nothing of value? Perhaps—if the client knows the risks, wants to push ahead, and agrees to pay for my efforts with full knowledge of what that means.

Or there may be circumstances where my work is laying the groundwork for considerable future value. For example, in a situation where multiple rounds of negotiation are not achieving the desired result, but may be breaking down the resistance of the other party, or may be laying the foundation on which a future agreement can be achieved. How do you determine that value? Should it be by the hour? Or some other measurement that you and the client agree upon?

Assessing outcome risk will also make me much more careful in deciding which files to take and how much time to invest in them. I may decide to take on a file with high upside and high risk for a client on the basis that we share the risk. Perhaps I'll set an estimate and we'll agree that I'll charge half the estimate if we lose and twice the estimate if we achieve the desired result.

Some lawyers and clients can see the immediate risk/reward where financial transactions are involved. Particularly in investment banking, clients are prepared to pay a premium if a deal closes and expect a discount if it fails. Similarly, contingent fees tied to litigation outcomes are common.

In classic litigation arrangements, hourly billing has reigned supreme for years. Though clients who lose a case are much more interested in negotiating down a bill than clients who win are prepared to pay more.

It makes logical sense to have a discussion with a client at the onset of a matter. Perhaps the lawyer has an idea for a novel argument that has never been tried, or a unique and unorthodox approach to a negotiation. If it succeeds and creates enormous value for the client, should the lawyer share in the reward? Presumably only if she is prepared to share the risk. The approach is entrepreneurial and aligns with client interests. We'll take a more careful look at this in *Triple F,* my upcoming book.

Some have argued that this type of approach means the lawyer can no longer be a completely objective advisor. I suggest that in many situations a client might want an objective overview, but also hope for a passionate representation of his interests.

These types of arrangements, at least for now, are not the norm. Even institutional in-house counsel, when offered alternative billing options tied to new models, tends to fall back on the billable hour (often at an agreed percentage discount).

The billable hour and young associates

If you've worked as a summer student in a large firm, you've been largely insulated from any of these issues. Once you begin life as a junior associate, life changes. Very often summer employment before articling is treated like summer camp: lots of bonding and social events, not a whole lot of work. Some firms are very careful to project that image: plenty of research for lawyers on their pet projects that's non-billable.

Once you move into the articling program and into first year, the gloves come off. Some of the major firms believe that the harder they work you, the more you will learn. Others believe their level of profitability is tied to getting the maximum number of billable hours from their associates. Often the Perality that they are fodder and must pay their dues by churning out hours of low-level work scares many smart young lawyers away from continuing in the profession.

When should your hourly rate change?

The industry norm is that a lawyer's hourly rate increases each year, based on the theory that with more experience they are becoming more efficient, more learned, and hence more valuable. Most firms coordinate the changes yearly on the anniversary of your hire, which is a bit unrealistic (and existing clients find it irritating), but it is the way the industry operates. Imagine walking into the grocery store tomorrow to see the following:

All items now 5 percent more. Happy anniversary, shoppers.

The rate hike covers law-firm overhead increases, but from a client perspective it's irrational. Your Perality is that once you become an expert in an area of law, you will be more valuable and more efficient, and your rate should be higher. Contrast that with a new area of law that you're just learning, which makes you less efficient. That should translate to a lower rate. The notion that you would have a single hourly rate that is automatically increased annually and is applicable to all matters (regardless of your expertise) needs to be challenged and reconsidered in light of the client's Perality.

If, now or later in your career you have control over your own rate, you might want to vary it by client and by area of experience, possibly even retainer by retainer. If you've negotiated an agreement to deal with this eventuality with the client, all the better. More about this on the section on retainers in the next chapter.

Remember, clients will pay a premium when there's a scarcity of talent that you have. For example, I engaged one former prime minister who was a genius at mediation. We did not bill him out by the hour; rather we charged hundreds of times more to deliver results that clients felt were fair.

In assessing any increase in your rate, you need to ask only one question before the client asks it:

Why am I more valuable to the client?

Delegation challenges

Institutional clients such as banks and insurance companies sometimes pose problems for young lawyers. Those clients have sophisticated billing software and will not accept time billed by students or, in some cases, first- or second-year lawyers, largely because their time spent, even at low hourly rates, is perceived to be inefficient. Darned Perality. Consequently, it's in the client interest that once you're trained to do a task, they will want you to repeat it over and over, because you'll be most efficient doing what you know, even at a higher hourly rate. Unfortunately for you, the only way you will learn and personally grow is if you pass on repetitive tasks to those more junior, while you take on new tasks and inefficiently learn how to do them. You're caught in a catch-22.

The irony is that the people in the institutions driving these policies were once in law firms and understood how important the training function is to the efficiency and health of the firm serving the client.

Billable hours get tracked at every level of the firm right up through the partners. In many firms if a partner's hours slip, their income will decline. Traditionally, more senior lawyers delegate tasks they're bored of doing to younger lawyers, who find the work interesting. However, if your firm's partners are feeling economic pressure or if overall workloads are slowing down, odds are that these more senior professionals may be avoiding delegation in order to pad their own statistics and protect their own compensation.

I interviewed one third-year lawyer who had come to hate his work at a prestigious downtown firm. He had become the firm's expert at preparing and filing a particular form with a particular government agency on complicated purchase transactions. On the one hand he was proud that he was the recognized expert. On the other hand…he was pigeonholed. Within a year he left to develop software solutions for the legal profession.

Now that we've taken a look at billable hours and their impact, it's time to learn how to understand the true measure of profitability, that is, converting the work into collected cash.

CHAPTER 14

Billing—From File Intake to Collection

There's a common misconception that sending a bill is the last thing you worry about on a new-client file. Just the opposite is true. You begin the process of selling yourself and your bill from the moment you meet a client. You also need to evaluate new clients from the moment you meet them to make sure all the work you're about to undertake can and will be paid.

From the retainer through file-intake decisions and executing the work, to sending and collecting the bill, you need a strategy for sizing up prospective clients and then understanding them. More important, you need to train yourself in establishing expectations, so that your client feels well-treated throughout. I can't tell you how many promising relationships have been ruined when the client is shocked by the first invoice for services. You're at an early stage in your career, so now is the perfect time to develop some good habits around opening files.

> *Set clear expectations on both sides, live up to your promises, and insist the client do the same.*

The term *retainer* has two meanings for lawyers. The first is the written agreement you enter into with the client before you commence work. The second is the amount of money you take in advance when you open the file. Let's look at these in reverse order.

The funding retainer

The sum of money in a retainer is an amount advanced in trust that you hold against future expenses. If you were a landlord, you'd think nothing of having a prospective tenant provide a cheque upfront for last month's rent. In other professions the advance has different names, but the principle is the same.

The retainer does not have to be a huge amount and will probably vary depending on whether the work involved is a small, midsize, or large matter. It doesn't take a business degree to recognize that if a client is reluctant to advance funds at the onset of a file, it's likely an indication of problems to come.

Don't be afraid to ask for a sufficient enough retainer as a credit check against your incoming client's solvency. If the prospective client balks at advancing funds, it's either a sign they do not value lawyers' services, or they are well intentioned but, in the words of Gilbert and Sullivan, "an impecunious party." At one point I insisted on a $5,000 minimum retainer for all new clients. It shortened the interview process for prospective clients who evidently had no money.[56]

My experience with lawyers is that so many feel uncomfortable asking a new client for money up front. Some lawyers feel uncomfortable *ever* asking for money. As the first of your clear expectations, set up how you plan to bill and how quickly you expect payment. Most lawyers are quite shy about setting these expectations. They fear that if they're too direct, the client may go somewhere else. I assure you, those clients who leave will eventually find someone else to do their work for free.

You may not always need a retainer. For example, if you're being tested on a small first matter from a large corporation, or if you have spent a year courting a particular prospect, you might decide to pass on the retainer and take the risk. As long as you have

---

56. Some larger firms will not accept new clients with matters worth less than $25,000 and in some cases more.

an open conversation with the client that details how often you'll be sending invoices (either monthly, or when a matter is completed, or at certain trigger events), and the expectation for terms of payment.

> *Are you the client's professional or the banker?*

Professionals who fail to adequately address how and when they are being paid inevitably become the financiers of their clients' affairs. The more time you spend chasing clients to get paid, the more interest you are paying to your own banker.

The retainer agreement

It's also necessary practice to begin each mandate with a written retainer agreement, which considers the following issues:

- What services are you going to provide?

- Are you billing by the hour? If so, at what rate?

- Can you withdraw in certain circumstances?

Various other issues must also be dealt with, but you should not be providing any legal advice without an agreement in place.

Every firm has a standard-form retainer letter that deals with a myriad of issues, including conflicts with other existing or potential clients.[57] Your local law society or bar association also has ample resources on its website. That said, if appropriate do not take this letter as a fixed precedent. As much as you can, tailor it to your client, your firm, your mandate, and any other important business issue.[58]

---

57. I'm deliberately not dealing with the issue of conflict checks, a matter you must take care of before accepting any mandate. Your local bar association can provide you with the relevant information.

58. Clients with in-house legal departments will often negotiate the retainer agreement, feeling it is too "one-sided" in favour of the law firm.

File-intake decisions and special situations

Practitioners at all ages and stages make the same mistake, one you would do well to avoid. They provide free advice to people who are not clients. There are various types of prospects to be particularly wary of: the "freebies," who are convinced they're entitled to some free advice before they decide whether to retain you; the "self-entitled" who believe professionals are rich and should do things (like help them) for free; and the "it's already in your computer system" types who are convinced all you have to do is push a button and out pops an agreement— to name a few.

Do *not* provide free advice. As soon as you provide any advice, you have created a relationship with the client. Your liability is engaged even if you're never paid a dime. If you are going to accept a *pro bono* matter, do so with your eyes open and treat it with the same respect that you would a billing file. Your *pro bono* respect and attention is not about wanting to be a nice or competent person, but because giving unregulated free advice is going to get you in trouble.

As a second-year lawyer I got a call from my aunt Doris because one of her work colleagues was in tears. The woman was an immigrant who was being hounded by the city over an apartment building she inherited from her husband. According to my aunt, the city was being malicious. Though I had no knowledge of municipal law, I spoke to the woman. Eugenia had a heavy European accent. She was crying about how the city was persecuting her, a poor widow.

After I made a couple of phone calls, I discovered her husband had been a slumlord and the city was about to condemn the building. The file went on forever, I never got paid, and most of the time I felt incompetent. But I took one key lesson from the debacle. If you are taking a matter *pro bono*, then make that clear decision at the start and document it. Restrict yourself to areas of competence. Do not fall into it because you were sloppy at the onset.

Alyssa Tomkins, the Ottawa based litigator I spoke with in Chapter 1, has spent a number of years figuring out how to manage having both paying and *pro bono* clients in a very thoughtful and strategic manner. Along with her heavy case load, she is managing two cases that are important to her personally: the first, a health-related case attempting to set aside a thalidomide class action settlement for victims who were not well served by the class; the second, a Charter of Rights challenge to the six-month sobriety requirement to obtain a liver transplant. These cases may not pay money, but they have translated to gold in other regards. Alyssa wants to build her public law profile, and these cases have led to speaking engagements and coverage by mainstream and social media. Other interventions on *pro bono* matters before the Supreme Court of Canada have provided invaluable experience and profile.

Should you take files on contingency?

A contingency file is one that pays only if you win. If you lose, however, you may end up with far less than nothing! Contingency files are worthwhile when the upside of winning is significant compared with the risk that the file may be lost or drawn out for years and years.

You must go into contingency work with your eyes wide open. If no litigation funder is available, the disbursements that you have to carry out of your own pocket can become overwhelming. My own rule of thumb was that these types of files should not take up more than about 3 to 5 percent of our overall practice. Yet some exclusive litigation firms thrive on them and have an impressive track record of settlements.[59]

59. Peter Angelos, a Maryland class action lawyer, once earned a fee of $150 million on a settlement of state litigation against tobacco companies. He is the majority owner of the Baltimore Orioles.

The Volkswagen emissions scandal settled for $290 million; RCMP harassment, $150 million. The courts limit the amount that can go to legal fees, but if one assumes a rate between 15 and 25 percent, the numbers add up quickly. More difficult to swallow is the settlement for residential school survivors at $1.9 billion (with a 15 percent limitation on lawyers' fees from the settlement added to the arrangement between lawyer and individual clients, up to another 15 percent). Thus a lawyer representing 1,000 class-victims, with an average settlement of $93,500, could have earned as much as $2.8 million, leading many client advocates to wonder about who was served by justice.

Do not mistake contingency for files that you work on hoping one day to make a modest profit, with an agreement to get paid your hourly rate or a fixed fee representing the value of all your time if you win. That is simply bad business. If you don't attach enough reward to your risk, you're making a sucker bet. Kind of like betting on the twenty-five-point NFL underdog at even odds.

When a client cannot pay

When I was running Heenan Blaikie, one of my former partners acted for clients in separation and divorce proceedings against their rich spouses. The expectation, on taking a file, was that one day the case would settle for one half of a large estate. More than enough to cover a very large legal bill that accumulated—in theory. In practice, these matters can be bitterly emotional, and in many cases the party with means exacted revenge by stretching the court proceedings for years, starving out a settlement. This meant we went years in some cases without being paid. Worse were cases where the client had to settle for a small amount in order to subsist, so we did not recover significant amounts of our billed time. We became the client's second banker—the one that had to write off the bad debt.

If you, like my former partner, feel a duty to represent the underdog or the underserved, set a limit on the percentage of your practice this will represent. You must also accept that you may not be paid for years, and sometimes far less than you anticipated at the outset. In long drawn-out battles, things rarely go according to plan.

Setting the budget

Most lawyers are thrilled to dive into work on a new matter. They run directly from executing the retainer agreement to digging right into the file. The joy in starting work on a file you've struggled hard to land is immeasurable. However, if you dig the hole before you've figured out its dimensions, you may fall into your grave. You've missed a critical step:

Don't start digging in until you've measured!

Sounds logical, doesn't it? At the outset of a matter, of course you should have a discussion with the client about its likely cost. To estimate the cost, you may need to spend a few hours assessing what the matter involves. Begin with your first estimate of the work—the number of steps to get from beginning to end, the process and the people who need to be involved—and then cost out the likely alternative scenarios. Then you need to meet with the client and take her through your process. Let her be your partner in deciding how to run the file and setting the budget for each step along the way, as well as how often you're going to be paid, so there are no misunderstandings later. Sounds logical, doesn't it? In my experience, few lawyers do it.

Some clients will insist on this type of discussion, while others will trust your estimate without question. But the ones you have to worry about the most are the ones who do not ask for any kind of estimate. Experience has taught me they are the most likely to complain.

The problem is that estimating the cost of a file depends on a number of factors outside your control. Here are a few examples: The lawyer on the other side may be unreasonable, and things that should take five hours take ten. Your own client may behave in unpredictable ways, or change his mind midway through the process, or surprise you by being intransigent on a matter where you believe that accommodation is the best strategy to find a solution within budget.

The most dangerous situations involve emotional clients who say they're willing to go to the end of the earth to pursue the matter, win or lose, until they do and find out how much the process cost them. When the costs exceed the benefits, clients tend to forget their emotional state and blame the person sending the bill.

Some clients will give you carte blanche. This is another group you need to worry about, particularly when they exhort, with emotion, "I don't care about the cost, it's about the principle." Anyone who tells you that should be handled with caution.

Eventually clients calm down and forget the discussion; or in a corporate setting, your contact leaves or is replaced. At that point guess who is holding the proverbial bag?

The art of setting the budget involves a few practicalities that should be discussed at the outset:

- What is the objective? To litigate or settle? To come to an agreement or to thwart it?

- Is there an important principle at play for the client organization?

- If it's a litigation matter, is it critical to the business or family, or not critical?

These are all points you need to understand before you touch your keyboard[60] for the first time on the matter. But you must also understand that objectives change with time, perspective, and shifting situations. As you will come to learn, success is grounded in keeping the lines of communication open from beginning to end. Make sure your changing reality is aligned with your clients' perceptions—Perality.

If you can come to consensus with the client on the true objectives, you will have a better idea of how to cost the file. But what happens when there are too many variables to set an accurate quote? Do you wait until you become more certain? That could take months or in some cases, years. That is not the time to defer the discussion. You need to do exactly the opposite.

Whether it's complex litigation that has many stages, a negotiation that might lead to litigation if the discussions break down, an intransigent party on the other side that has to be outwaited or outlasted, or the possibility of a subsequent event that changes the perspective, your initial quote may prove difficult to estimate.

In those cases, break the file down into components. Explain that there are a number of forks in the road along the way. Cost out best and worst case for each fork. In other words, break the file into

---

60. In the olden days of the past century, the idiom was "lift your pen."

segments, from beginning to end, with its best-case and worst-case scenarios—then give the client the variable costs. Help them to decide, with you, which alternatives they prefer.

> *Make the client a partner in the costing process.*

If you are working with in-house counsel, befriend them. They are allies. But be wary, as your single in-house contact can also become a veil hiding a whole different reality in the C-suite. A Perality trap. In other words, the counsel may appreciate you but has not done a good job of explaining your value to the people who will be approving the bill.

As I mentioned earlier, regular visits to the client's office may allow you to get to know not only the counsel but the business people calling the shots. If the matter is large enough, coordinate with the in-house to make sure you have sufficient access to the person who needs to understand the value you are delivering. Usually that is the person who has to approve the bill.

Review the projections against the actuals regularly. For some clients a monthly assessment is in order; for others it could be quarterly. Use it as an excuse to touch base or meet with the client. Don't let long periods of time go by during which you're accumulating significant billable hours. You need to be worried in those situations that the client's perception is that everything is under control and on budget when it's not. Communicate early. Communicate often. Explain and agree on direction, scope, and cost. Review and revise regularly.

If, for example, you explain to a client that defending a wrongful termination suit can go one of four ways with variable cost alternatives, the client may very well build the costs into their strategy at the outset. If the facts change, or the unpredictable occurs, then immediately communicate with the client and explain the impact on costing the services either up or down. Providing these alternatives may also assist the client in determining when and whether to settle.

Experience tells us that regardless of how much a client wants to win a file at the onset, when the legal costs exceed what they would have paid the opposing party to go away on day one of the process, you may not get paid in full—or worse, never see another file from that client.

Living with estimates

My friend George K. was telling me about a recent episode with his mechanic. He brought his car in for servicing at Lou's Garage on Adelaide Street.

"When I went to pick it up, the service rep told me to sit down," George said. I could hear the irritation in his voice. "Never a good sign. He tells me that while doing the repair, they found a crack in the camshaft. I don't even know what a camshaft is. Another eighteen-hundred bucks. Can you believe it?"

"He didn't call you to clear it in advance?"

"He told me he tried but couldn't reach me. He was sure I would say yes."

"Why do you keep going back?"

"It's my Uncle Lou."

I would never use Uncle Lou. Nor would you. The expectation is that if the camshaft issue comes up, you will get a call and provide an approval for the extra work.

When it comes to professional services, so many are just like Uncle Lou. They are uncomfortable, complacent, or just too lazy to make that call to revise the estimate. Yet it seems so obvious what you need to do: communicate immediately. Outline the options to the client. Let the client decide. Many lawyers do just the opposite. They do their best work on the file, putting off the uncomfortable extra-cost discussion until it's time to send the bill. They simply pray that Perality will not prey on them.

I can give you one additional piece of advice based on experience: If you quote $10,000 and bill $8,000, you may have a client for life. If you quote $10,000 and bill $12,000 with a series of well-meaning excuses, you may not have a client tomorrow.

What to do when things go off track

One young lawyer I mentor, Taylor, left on vacation during a lull in the negotiations for a new client, Estella DeVille, CEO of Dalmatian Designs. Estella had been negotiating a distribution agreement for North America for her specialized spotted rugs. Unfortunately, something came up and a new, revised draft was needed. Taylor decided to process the final sets of changes on his iPad while sitting beside the pool at Lake George. Big mistake. The technology for making corrections to the key agreement created a nightmare involving at least a dozen hours of vacation time spent on the file. Taylor figured he was a hero, working through his hard-earned vacation. Though had he thought to bring his laptop, those hours would have been conserved. The iPad just couldn't handle the stress.

When Estella received the bill, she reminded Taylor of the screw-up. Embarrassed, Taylor immediately offered her a courtesy discount.

Smart move on Taylor's part, but I explained over coffee that this was a missed opportunity. Taylor made the client raise the discomfort over the size of the bill by sending it out before first discussing it with her. While she praised him for working through his vacation (creating positive goodwill), Taylor took a risk. Instead, he might have called Estella upon return from vacation, apologizing for the screw-up, reminding her that he put her ahead of the vacation and offering an immediate discount for the technology problems. Perhaps Estella would have been thrilled with Taylor's dedication and might have agreed to pay the entire bill (or at least most of it). Same result and huge positive goodwill—no risk.

Docketing and billing

This brings us to the part of practice that's most difficult to master. It's so easy to screw up, and so filled with potential for conflict. I'm speaking of preparing, sending, and collecting accounts. It sounds simple. Do the work, send the bill, make sure the client pays you promptly. On bigger files, send accounts on a regular basis as the matter proceeds.

Many professionals believe that the task of preparing the bill is begun and completed once the work is done. They see billing as the dreadful work that follows all the fun on a challenging file or the nightmare on a file where nothing has gone according to plan. If you asked most lawyers, they'd admit that other than keeping track of their hours, billing is the part of the practice they enjoy the least.

Is it likely that some mentor is going to teach you early in your career what you really need to know about billing? Or firm finances generally? Given the general disaffection associated with the mere idea of billing, probably not. More likely, the office administrator will walk into your office one day and explain the firm policies and how to use the firm billing software. If you're in sole practice, you'll learn those mechanics quickly if you want to survive.

Walied Soliman, the chair of Norton Rose Fulbright Canada, spoke to me about the first client he ever billed as a young lawyer. The experience stayed with him for his entire career. Good or bad, we always remember our first time being entirely responsible for a client. It was a basic incorporation and he was very concerned about explaining the bill—$1,300 was a big number in the day. During the process of the entire file he obsessed over performing the tasks in the minimum number of hours to keep the bill as reasonable as possible.

"I think it's so important for young lawyers to take billing responsibility as early in their career as possible," Walied says. "It teaches responsibility for your time and responsiveness to your clients. Those are habits that can only be developed if you know you are the person who has to defend the cost to the client."

Keeping track of your time sounds simple enough, but if the file does not lend itself to being billed every month, when you finally bill it, months may have passed since your earliest time entries. Here's a classic I've seen many clients complain about: "22 May 2019: 2 hours—worked on file." That's the type of time entry made by a lawyer relying on the client not to review the bill.

Instead, edit each entry as if you were the one paying the bill. Live the client's Perality. Can they read it and immediately justify it? Better still, record the details right away after doing the work. Remembering what actually happened in those two hours on 22 May 2019 after a week or two, or three, have passed is downright impossible.

The above is just one example of terrible habits in time recording. There will always be excuses: You're so busy working that you don't have time to record the time or the file number. You're flip-flopping between phone calls and you'll write it all down later. Or you decide you'll figure out all your docketed time over the weekend. The worst offenders sit down at month end, going entry by entry in their calendar to figure out what they did. Those lawyers should be writing fiction. I can barely remember what I had for lunch last Tuesday, much less try to remember whom I spoke to over the phone and what the subject was.

Most firm administrators will insist that you record your time entries using the appropriate software, which connects to your computer and phone. The software is designed to make your life simpler and more efficient. Over time many lawyers unhook themselves, worrying that the system is not fair to the client, capturing both efficient and inefficient time. In other words, the system may assume you're working even when you're on a break, daydreaming, or hopping between emails.

Here's the problem in most law firms. You have a sense of the value of your work. It's taking much longer than you expected, or if the work was delegated to you, more time than what you perceive the senior lawyer who handed you the work may have estimated. So you engage in the process known as "self-editing." Some senior lawyers give you a nudge and a wink, encouraging you not to enter all your hours, even if the firm policy requires you to. This is an unfortunate byproduct of the billable hour. No one wants to be badly judged by some firm committee on their inefficient use of time. So better not to record the time than to write it off.

The whole thing is irrational when you consider that junior lawyers who are learning are supposed to be inefficient. Why do you think your hourly rate is lower than a more senior lawyer's? How else do you learn? What's the difference between an hour not spent and an hour not recorded? What's wrong with writing off hours that are of no value to clients? These are questions that the industry continues to grapple with.

More importantly, what can you learn from all this? Here's my perspective as a former managing partner of hundreds of lawyers. When it's your turn to take responsibility for a file, you must learn to estimate what you think it should cost the client, communicate that clearly, and then live with it. If facts or circumstances change, you deal with it. The process of docketing time is designed to give you an idea how long it takes you to accomplish tasks and whether you're becoming more efficient with repetition. You can't do that if you are self-editing.

Preparing the invoice

Frank Ramos is the managing partner of Clarke Silverglate in Miami, Florida, and has been providing advice to young professionals for many years. His advice on billing best summarizes the key points as well as anything I've ever read:

- Be precise, detailed, and informative with your entries.

- Docket as you go. Don't wait until the end of the day, and certainty not the end of the week or month.

- Your entries should tell a story about your file. The client should read your entries and know the story of her case or matter.

- Entries should explain not only the task but why it was performed. If you create an entry addressing research you did, explain why you did it.

- When making any entry, ask yourself: if you were the client, would you pay for it?

- Proofread for grammar, typos, and misspellings.

Progress billing

If the file is ongoing, the lawyer should send progress bills along the way. Some firms insist that bills be sent to the client monthly—but some of those bills go out the door without being reviewed all that carefully. Which is fine if no one is reading the invoice when it arrives! But if the client actually cares about what he's paying for … do I need to explain what comes next?

I had a recent experience as a client of a large firm that handled a matter for me. The day the file was completed—a month ago—I would have paid the bill immediately, I was so enchanted with the service. As time lags and I still haven't received a bill, I begin to wonder what their problem is. If they wait another month or two or more, the goodwill lags. They're also sending me a message: they don't care that much about speed of payment. They run the risk that their invoice goes to the bottom of my to-do list.

I know it's counter-intuitive, but **sending clients prompt and detailed bills is a sign you care about them.** Offering to discuss the draft bill with them before you go final also goes toward cementing your partnership.

In some cases, disbursement recording lags and creates a hold-up. Understand that some clients, particularly public companies, are judged by their quarterly reporting. If their third quarter cost gets reported in the fourth quarter because you failed to get your bill out in time, guess who's going to have a problem?[61] Rather than holding back a ten-thousand-dollar bill over an eighteen-dollar delivery charge, you might want to let the client know that in sixty days there may be a separate invoice for any late-entered costs.

Payment—sooner or later

If a client agrees to pay monthly within thirty days of invoice and you're providing ongoing service, then enforce his end of the bargain if he's late. There are few situations worse than when the client begins to pay later, and later, and later, and your monthly bills pile up unpaid. Yet this happens more often than you would imagine. Remember you're the lawyer, not the banker. The more regularly you

61. In most cases if you can't get your bill out in time, you can solve their reporting problem by confirming the amount of the bill that pertains to the quarter and indicating that the bill will follow shortly.

bill and collect, the less your own need to borrow while your line of credit pays your employees and your draws.

Larger institutions, which you might expect would be in a position to pay sooner, often insist on 90-to-120-day credit on their bills and don't really give you an option. In cases like these, monitor them carefully to be sure they're abiding by the payment terms. Often several calls to the accounts payable clerk are necessary; otherwise, a computer glitch can send your invoice spinning through institutional purgatory to end up in your 120- to 180-day unpaid receivable pile. Not good news for your credit line at the bank.

> *Getting bills paid in a timely manner is part of your job and your duty to yourself.*

It is so easy to dig a hole for yourself if you haven't managed the client communication well. For some reason, a client who'd be more than prepared to pay $8,000 per month for a year will be outraged if you give her free credit for the year and then send a $96,000 bill. You'll have failed in helping her manage her own budgeting.

A better perspective on billing and collection

Some lawyers are masters of billing. Their clients are thrilled to pay the accounts. No amount is too large.[62] Those lawyers operate on a completely different premise. They reject the notion that billing is the last thing to take care of. *That idea is dead wrong.* Smart lawyers begin the billing process at the moment of introduction to a new client or at the onset of a new file from an existing client. Not at the end. What do I mean?

---

62. That is hyperbole, except for very large transactions with investment bankers, who are passing along the bill to their clients—as long as the deal closes!

Let's turn the approach to billing on its head:

From the moment of inception, you need to sell your bill and explain everything it's paying for. Once again, it's about communication. As the client outlines the problem, your job is to explain all the services that she'll be getting for the bill, including, among a host of other issues specific to the matter at hand —

- the strategy to deal with the problem,

- the value you can add in arriving at the solution,

- the length of time it may take (factoring in issues such as who the opponent is, what the other party's options might be, and what the client's key business objectives are),

- the importance of the matter to the client's business,

- the client's timeline objective, and

- the achievability of their desired outcome.

To be clear, I'm not suggesting you walk into the first meeting with the intent of having all the answers. Your job is to ask the right questions, take a 360-degree look at the impact of the matter on the client's business or life, slowly gather information, and then communicate a plan of attack along with a sense of cost.

As more information becomes available, your job is to lead, to assess and reassess, and to communicate as new facts impact your original assessment. You're continually revising the attack plan and the budget, making your client your partner in the process.

Occasionally the professionals representing the adverse party are unreasonable or impossible to deal with. I used to call them LFH (Lawyers From Hell). The LFH can wreak havoc on your estimates. Once you've discovered one on the other side, communicate that to your client and revise your estimates.

This is quite similar to all the rest of your client issues, but this is the one that involves money—it impacts you personally. Difficult conversations about changes in cost may be required as new information presents itself. It's the reason many lawyers shy away from those discussions, waiting for the unresolved cost issue to blow up in their faces at the very end.

A case study of Perality and billing

Every lawyer I know has a battle story about clients who blanched at a bill. I recall one in particular when an investment bank hired us to replace their incumbent counsel on a critical piece of litigation. The case was of strategic importance, and they were unhappy with the work of the other firm. A dream come true for us: a chance to impress.

When the file arrived, the case prospects looked dim, but due to ingenious litigation strategy we won. The bill was over $100,000—half what they had previously spent without any result. We expected the client to be thrilled and use us on all their future litigation: our Perality. Instead they complained that the bill was outrageously high: their Perality.

While we delivered a fantastic result, where had we failed? It was pretty simple. The client was not kept up to date on the cost. Had we said upfront, "Here's the battle plan based on how important this case is for your reputation. Please understand that the cost will be as much as one hundred thousand dollars," the client might have gulped, but they would have made a strategic/cost decision. Then if the litigators had delivered a bill for $90,000, the client might have been thrilled that it came in $10,000 under the expectation.

Experience tells us billing is an art, not a science. Like everything else in practice, it's based on managing client expectations, predicting what may go wrong, confronting the unexpected as it arises, and having candid discussions with clients about how to navigate issues *together in partnership,* along with delivering crisp, effective, timely service. Ultimately it all comes down to communication. Surprise! Invest the time in understanding the process and the strategy. Then communicate. At the end of the day, you reap what you sow.

Value for service

This chapter has taken you through the conventional approach to billing management, but has avoided discussion of a fundamental problem at the core of hourly billing. Somewhere along the lifeline of the billable hour, most legal professionals have lost sight of the value proposition for clients. It goes something like this:

The work I am doing has a value for the client, and is not necessarily tied to the amount of time I spend on it. If I need to spend $25,000 of billable time on a matter that is delivering minimal advantage to the client, am I going to have a satisfied client? Isn't it best to have that discussion in advance? Sometimes the value to the client of that $25,000 of time investment is immeasurable. Sometimes it's a complete waste.

Emotional clients often want immediate, strong, irreversible action, regardless of cost. Months later, when they calm down, they realize that the cost completely outweighs the benefit and they try to negotiate the bill down. Mostly they are upset with you for not controlling the costs, for going way over the original budget, conveniently forgetting they pushed you every step of the way. Easier to blame you than themselves.

Sometimes effective push-back at each step along the path and a reminder of the cost increase is exactly the medicine the client needs in those situations. Of course, if push-back fails and the client refuses to heed your advice to settle or come to a quick agreement, send the client a note explaining why you've advised against the expensive course of action they're taking. Eventually it will come in handy.

In-house litigation departments are sometimes the worst offenders. Particularly if the head of the department has handed off a matter to a younger lawyer without instruction other than, "Here is the outside counsel we work with." The young lawyer retains you and asks you to "take care of it." If you have not asked the following questions, you are setting yourself up for problems later on:

- Does the case concern an important principle?

- If not, why spend a fortune on proceedings?

- Is the intention to drag it out or settle?

- Is there an internal budget constraint that you should know about before you work out your strategy?

The lawyer who fails to invest the time upfront on these issues is courting problems later on. The ostrich defence rarely succeeds in court or as a billing tactic.

Artificial intelligence and billing

With the developing AI in particular industries, some of the above issues may disappear over the next few years. The advent of predictive software that scans a data bank of court awards and settlements and can make reliable prediction of likely outcomes will be a big time-saver if strategically used by outside counsel. For example, an insurance company processing claims can use software to feed in the type of injury and its medical consequences and find out in thirty seconds what the reasonable range of settlement should be, based on all previous settlements and court decisions.

When there is no AI to assist, then discussion, reason, and judgment need to prevail.[63] Quiz your client on their business objectives in a litigation before taking the costly step of moving from filing proceedings to lengthy discovery, endless motions, and failed mediations.

> *Don't simply take instructions and go.*

With experience, hard work and strong communication skills, you will become better at predicting likely outcomes.

---

63. Once upon a time we labelled this "human intelligence."

When hourly billing makes no sense

The flip side of the value proposition is also worthy of reflection. Take the case where in about five hours of work because of my specialized expertise or connections, I can advance the client's business by over one million dollars. Should I be billing $2,500 for that? If you're operating on a standard retainer agreement with standard hourly rates (assuming your billing rate is $500/hour), you will be stuck.

Where the situation permits a negotiation of value billing with a client, do not shy away. If you can convince the client that you will both be more effective if you are aligned, then together you can assess likely outcomes and fee structures that address success. That then opens the door for your five hours' time to be valued at so much more.

I spent a career pioneering value for service at my firm. I rarely billed by the hour, believing it to be inefficient. Most of my clients agreed up front as to what would be fair compensation for a desired result.

The billable hour is quite handy when you have a client who literally does not care what the file costs and with whom you expect to generate considerable work over a length of time. But these clients are rare, other than at the upper end of the profession.

My final point takes us back to the beginning—the value of the billing hour. To me, the notion that an hour of legal service is worth anything of value, much less the arbitrary hourly rate that is set and agreed to, is itself a colossal delusion. It is the delusion that powers an entire industry and has done so for over half a century. It built an entire industry, but how much longer will it last in a rapidly changing business environment? Will you be the one bold enough to topple the Colossus? Can you adjust your marketing strategy with new clients? Think about replacing the billable hour with a different approach to delivering and billing for your services—and create a new Perality.

CHAPTER 15

Are You Well Suited to Work In-house?

So many lawyers wonder early in their career if they should be working in-house for a corporation or business instead of in private practice. Not an easy decision, regardless of the moment in your career you decide to make the jump. I've canvassed a number of in-house leaders with a view to giving you some idea of what life is like on the inside of an organization and what you might expect.

Learning the business

The one point every in-house lawyer emphasizes is that you are part of a team that is counsel to a business. David Goldman, in-house counsel for a real estate development and construction business, winner of a Lexpert Zenith award and three-time nominee for Canadian General Counsel of the Year, put it quite succinctly:

"You really have to understand the business you're serving. You can't just get by on legal expertise. You have to apply your legal judgment and practical skills when the company is making hard business decisions."

The best lawyers are able to help their clients understand and assess the risk of taking a course of action. That requirement is magnified when you're working for the business.

Erin O'Toole, who spent a number of years at Proctor & Gamble, tells of how the CEO of the company insisted his lawyers understand all the product lines of the company. His advice to others: "Make sure you know enough about the business outside your direct level of responsibility."

Ben Westelman is even more emphatic. Ben left the partnership track a few years ago to take a senior in-house position with eBay, joining its fast-growing online classifieds business. He is responsible from his base in Canada for direct reports in a number of different countries globally. Most of the workings of the group are tied to a deep understanding of the business. "The advice we give has to be practical, not theoretical. We have to focus on getting to a solution."

It's not enough to isolate a problem and wait for someone on the business side to make the decision. "The legal team has to always realize that there is an opportunity cost to the business of not taking a decision." All the general counsel I've interviewed agree that they need to understand the financial issues, the metrics that matter to the business, and the strategy before they can weigh in with legal advice.

This means that to succeed in-house, you have to expand your reach beyond the law and into business.

"The further you broaden your horizons, the more likely you are to be valuable." That's the advice of Mark Le Blanc, who describes himself as a business-minded lawyer and who runs a large team of lawyers and other professionals. TVO's business model made a sharp left turn a few years ago, and Mark had to become nimble and learn about many areas of which he had no previous knowledge. He was involved in a team effort with business leaders of the company to shepherd the government-owned conventional broadcaster into the digital age.

Plus-shaped lawyers

Mark touts the benefits of becoming what he calls "plus-shaped" lawyers.[64] Look at the + sign. The bottom of the vertical line of the + represents your legal abilities, which you'll continue to develop with experience. The top half of the vertical represents the soft skills one

---

64. For a more thorough examination of the plus-shaped lawyer and its forerunner, the T-shaped lawyer, see https://bit.ly/3f8QNjk.

needs to survive, which include interpersonal skills, empathy, listening skills, questioning skills, judgment, and other qualities tied to your emotional intelligence rather than your intellect. We have considered the development of these skills in earlier chapters.

The horizontal axis represents the skills you bring to the practice from the rest of your life or your studies outside the practice of law. Those include technology, business, project management, financial reporting and budgets, industrial relations or human resources, data security, risk management, politics, data analysis—the list goes on. As Mark puts it, "If all you know is the law, without any other skills that will be helpful in the business environment, you're not doing yourself any favours."

I ask Mark if he believes a business degree gives candidates an edge.

"MBA students have studied process management, which is becoming critical in terms of how to manage tasks in our legal department efficiently. The legal and business units are so intertwined that you can't give effective legal advice without a thorough knowledge of the business impact."

Mark gives an example. "Take our contract management systems. We license all kinds of shows and we've set up a system where the day a licence agreement is signed, the business people *just* have to fill in the blanks on a form. The information gets inputted into the software system. That way we know the term and payment dates, and our software will remind us when renewal notices have to be given. The only problem is that our internal clients are so busy, they *forget* to enter the information. Many of them just weren't using it."

"So, the legal group has created this system that only works in theory?" I ask.

"Exactly," Mark says. "The lawyers have to learn that it's not enough to set up a technology system and simply hand it off to the business unit. First the legal department has to sell the value proposition of the proposal at the C-suite of the company. Then they need to go out into the rest of the organization and teach people how and when to use it. With the backing of the executives in the C-suite, selling becomes easier. Once all that is done, the lawyers have to come up with a process to enforce it so that it works for the business team."

It all sounds so obvious, but all too often lawyers give their client contacts instructions without any idea if the advice is being implemented.

"If you're going to be effective working in-house," Mark says, "quite frankly, you need to sell your value and how you can help the business unit achieve their organizational objectives."

Jennifer Pollock of Ratehub.ca sees those other skills as critical to her own success. "I'm at a high growth company, with a lot of interesting people. We've tripled in size since I joined them four years ago. The role of the group that I manage is to catch everything that slips through the cracks having to do with risk management, compliance, and finance." Not an easy task in a business that continues to evolve.

"Most important," she says, "my role involves ensuring the systems and processes that have been put in place are continually adapted to make sure they work for an evolving business. Three quarters of my job has nothing to do with my accounting skills, so I had to build a team to complement my own skill set. Though I am very well served by the skills I developed producing musicals at Queen's University: process management and personnel skills, choosing the right people for the right positions to support me, working tight time lines, and bringing the musical from concept to reality. All far more valuable on many days than my accounting knowledge."

Wayne Levin joined Lionsgate, the big LA film studio, before it became Lionsgate. Eventually he was promoted up the ranks to the position of general counsel and chief strategic officer until his retirement a few years ago. Wayne sets out five critical questions he used when deciding to hire someone into his group, which factored into the success of in-house lawyers who worked for him:

1. Had they researched the company before the interview?

2. Did they demonstrate an eagerness to learn?

3. Did they have a background of team working experience or at least a willingness to be part of a team?

4. Did they understand that advancement is earned and not a right?

5. Did they possess the critical instinct to question how things are done?

A number of young lawyers express the belief that work-life balance might be better in-house than in private practice. The notion that you don't have to go out and market yourself, build a client base, keep track of your hours, or network suggests you'll have more time for a balanced life. But that is probably a function of the group you join. Perhaps within some huge institutions, like insurance companies, that may be the case. Perhaps not.

The general counsel I have spoken to remind me that getting to the "next level," wherever you are working, is a product of sacrifice, commitment, and hard work. If you worked in Wayne Levin's group at Lionsgate, you worked your tail off. The company was on an acquisition binge for fifteen years as they swallowed up and integrated companies both large and small. Presumably that's a fact you would have learned before your first interview, but the culture of growth, inventiveness, and camaraderie tied to stress and tough deadlines either spoke to you or frightened you away.

There is no easy path to the top—regardless of where the mountain is located. Ultimately, it's about choices. We'll look at some of those choices further on.

CHAPTER 16

If You Want It, Measure It

Peter Drucker, the famous Harvard business professor, has moulded the thoughts of a generation of business leaders across North America. He famously noted that "if you can't measure it, you can't manage it." This goes for business and for organizations, and it also has critical importance for your career.

Whether you're a student, associate, or aspiring in-house counsel, you need to have not only a sense of where you want to be a year or two from now but also a longer-range plan, even though that long-range plan will change annually as you become wiser and are exposed to more experiences and opportunities.

Are you going to sit in your office for the next seven or eight years, churning out the work and hoping for the best? If you're in a firm, are you expecting someone to walk into your office and tell you what you need to do next to advance your career? Take a look down the hallway at some of the seventh- and eighth-year associates. Steadily busy on files provided by others. Steadily going nowhere. Probably no more efficient than the cheaper fourth-year professionals coming up behind them. Headed for the exit and they don't yet realize it.

Do you want to be them? Or are you going to take charge of your future? So many firms expect that one day you'll wake up and just start doing it, as if you've absorbed your new-found initiative through the air-filtration system.

As my own career evolved, my focus on the long term was directed by how things were going in a particular year. By my fifth year of practice, though, my longer-term goals were becoming clearer.

Each year I would sit down and divide my objectives for the coming year into a number of categories. Then I would make a list of my priorities. There was nothing terribly sophisticated about my list. The only real question was whether I would have time to get to everything.

In that critical fifth year while I was working in Montreal, I wrote down one goal that changed the entire course of my career: "As an insurance policy, write the bar transfer exams to qualify in Ontario." It took me a year to get to it and required all kinds of coordination of work, study, and family schedules, but I managed to squeeze it in. If I hadn't prioritized it, however, it would have gotten lost in the shuffle of all my other priorities.

Two years after I made that notation, I walked into Peter Blaikie's office and told him I was prepared to open Heenan Blaikie in Toronto as an experiment. When I wrote the transfer exams, I had no such plan. But Quebec politics had changed, in my opinion for the worse. I knew I had to leave and the groundwork had been prepared.

Six months after that I began to set five-year plans, not just for my career, but for my burgeoning social experiment—a law firm with a new model for practising law, where having fun was a basic cultural value.[65] The five-year plan was aspirational. It gave me a long-term goal to shoot for—the stars. I also kept my one-year objectives in the forefront. You can't count to five unless you start with one. You can't meet a long-term objective unless you break it down into bite-size pieces.

Because I had set the time aside to consider where I wanted to be a year earlier, it was considerably easier to find the changes of route along the way and react to changes and situations that presented themselves. It's much easier to have an eye open for new opportunities when your mindset is keyed to look for them. That can only happen when you're keeping an eye out for the future.

I can't tell you how to devise your own plan, but here is a quick sample from earlier this year:

---

65. If you want to know more about that experiment, see *Breakdown: The Rise and Fall of Heenan Blaikie*, https://amzn.to/2LVkXv6

Norm's One-year Plan—March 2020

1. Survive

- Isolate during COVID-19

- Cancel all speaking engagements and convert to virtual meetings

2. Writing Projects

- Complete outline for handbook for young professionals

- Devote two months to a complete rewrite of second novel

- Send novel out for final edit

- While novel is out for final edit, take rough outline for handbook and begin writing

- Set up interviews with professionals

- Complete acceptable draft and engage editors to revise

- Send out draft for comments

- Send out draft to industry leaders for comment

3. Marketing

- Find an online course to learn how to market novel online

- Demystify Facebook and Amazon ads

- Fourth quarter reach out to all legal media outlets

4. Mentoring

- Continue LinkedIn postings

- Experiment with live mentoring on LinkedIn and/or Facebook in fourth quarter

5. Speaking Engagements

- Seek out book clubs

- Reach out to young professionals online and volunteer for Zoom engagements

- Connect with CBA, local organizations, and universities

Am I going to hit every item on this list before year end? Probably not, but I look at this list at least once every quarter to measure my progress. I've already adjusted it three times. If I'm able to check off everything on my list in the year, then my list is deficient. If I don't have a list that forces me to push, I won't accomplish half of what I'm capable of.

You may wonder what happens when circumstances beyond your control intervene to upset the plan. That's when the adage of poet Robbie Burns must be heeded: *"The best laid plans of mice and men gang oft aglay."*

Put in more modern terms: sh*t happens. Move on, rewrite the plan, and keep going as soon as you're able. Adjust and adapt. Reprioritize but never stop.

If you can keep one of these lists on your laptop in Word or Excel and amend and update it periodically, you'll be able to follow the progression and see it better. You'll understand how much you're driving forward with the objectives you've outlined and whether you're succeeding with initiative. Remember, riffing off Professor Drucker, if you don't measure your progress, you won't be efficient in moving ahead.

If you're looking for a downloadable form to make your plan you can get one on my website: *normanbacal.com.*

> *Write it down. Hold yourself to it. Make it happen.*

The last words: imagine and think

The most important thing you can do for yourself is to periodically set aside time to use your imagination. Some advertising agencies set aside an hour a day, doors closed, phones powered off, computers shut, so that their creative minds have some time to do nothing but think. Whether it's to consider your future, a problem on a file that resists solutions, a creative approach to a new file, or a novel idea, you have to set aside some time regularly to think. Unplug and shut down the devices sucking the attention span out of your brain, so you can ponder and let your imagination take you to new ideas and solutions. Some professionals are well liked because of their ability to execute. The ones who are beloved combine creativity and ingenuity and take the time to imagine things differently from the way they are.

CHAPTER 17

Career Switch

How do you know when it's time to make a move from where you are to the next stage of your journey? Ideas have changed dramatically in the past few years, particularly as they relate to the notion of sticking it out where you are. Almost no one believes that as a working theory any more. Most of you reading this assume that you'll have multiple jobs and experiences.

The goal is to enrich yourselves, to find meaning in your work, to grow as a person, rather than my generation's philosophy, which held that work and life values had little connection to one another.

I believe I built a law firm more in line with today's philosophy. Some critics believe I was too far ahead of my time, not profitable enough to survive. Too soft. Too inspired by the social relevance of the workplace. Did it matter who was right? I cared that my work philosophy matched my life philosophy. We are here to make a difference and to create a work environment where everyone matters, where everyone is excited to get up in the morning to expand on yesterday's accomplishments. I may no longer be running a law firm, but my life philosophy has not changed.

I'm hoping the comments that follow give you pause to think about how you can apply these lessons to the next steps in your careers. There are no hard and fast rules. What follows are some ideas and examples of what has worked in my experience.

Harvey Corn the contrarian

I was at a dinner as a second-year lawyer when the fellow sitting next to me recounted his story. At the same firm since he was a student, now a senior partner, he told me, "I decided to stick it out while all of my friends checker-boarded, trying the next "thing," more anxious in getting ahead at the next place, rather than putting their heads down and working through the dull days. I look around and I'm so far ahead of all of them. More important, as I developed, opportunities I could never have imagined presented themselves." Harvey Corn's advice would smack as outdated in the context of 2020.

However, it was advice I took to heart every time I thought about leaving Heenan Blaikie for something else. It worked out for me. I experienced multiple careers behind my desks: tax lawyer, film finance lawyer, corporate director of a multinational company, law firm builder, law firm leader. Today, author, also spawned by my thirty-five years at the same place. Except it was never the same place. It evolved and changed with me and my evolving world view. Are there situations today where it still might be good advice to follow?

Jennifer Lee points out to me in our interview, that in the modern economy, multiple careers are becoming the norm. "You're the exception, Norm, and a little outdated in the notion that it's possible to have many careers under the same roof. With the pace of change in the world, we all need to expect to have multiple careers, which means that every two or three years you need to imagine forward. Ask yourself, what new skills do I need to learn for my next career? That is the essence of the new economy."

When I point out to Jennifer that she's been at Deloitte for twelve years, she reminds me, "I had to be very entrepreneurial to stay here that long. I continue to ask myself how I modify my existing skill set to reset my personal strategic plan."

The short answer to this quandary is that only you can decide. Only you can be in charge of your future and the moves you make to increase your experience and more important, to experience your relevance.

Other career routes

Perhaps Hugo Alves is at the other end of the spectrum. He had evolved backward from one of the most famous lawyers on the globe in emissions trading to nobody. The fear we all live with. Rather than give up, feel sorry for himself, or fit in to the status quo of his firm, he sought the next dream, developing an expertise and team in what he hoped would become the next great wave: cannabis. His expertise extended well beyond the legal. He applied so many of the lessons outlined in this book that he could easily be its poster boy. He wrote, he spoke, he learned every aspect of the business, from growers and suppliers to service industries and financing. He met with anyone and everyone when they were still nobodies, before the industry was legalized and while it was evolving. He was evolving once more. Eventually he realized he knew as much about the cannabis business as anyone in the world.

When the unsolicited call came to join and lead a company expanding in the field, he took the next step, away from the security of partnership at his law firm. "*I took a massive pay cut, in exchange for a dream of massive upside.* Before I did so I asked myself the critical question: If I am unwilling to take this risk under these circumstances, then under what circumstances would I ever make a move? If not now, was I prepared to limit my horizons to partner in a law firm?"

That is a question each of us needs to ask individually, based on our circumstances, approach, and personality. Hugo acted on what he perceived was right for him.

Hugo's analysis was similar to Ben Westelman's, which led him from partnership at Gowlings to a senior in-house position at eBay. Ben listened to the inner voice urging him to take a chance in an area in which he was deeply interested. He felt ready for a new career challenge.

Christina Porretta followed a more circuitous path to her current position of GC at BDO. She clerked at the Federal Court of Appeal, took a position as a litigator, and discovered it was not for her. So she sought out a research position with a law firm that evolved into a ten-year stint at the firm that became Dentons Canada. She found the experience at Dentons satisfying, but she'd been wondering if there could be more, perhaps a new unwritten chapter. An unsolicited call led to her next move, a move which was set up by her growth at Dentons. BDO Canada represented a chance to test new skills—a chance to continue learning and begin building. A vital next step in her personal growth.

Aaron Friewald was a journalist and author turned lawyer. His own sense of independence led to him leaving a litigation boutique to open his own firm, with a couple of partners where they make all the rules…or don't.

Lorene Nagata was looking to switch litigation law firms when she felt there had to be something more to the practice of law. The search firm made her an unexpected offer to join them. That led, in turn, to her having the guts to go out and open her own shop. Could she ever have imagined it when she began to practice? You know the answer.

Erin O'Toole knew from the start that public service was in his blood. Along the road he learned as much as he could about the law and about practising law at a major corporation, then at a law firm, while he prepared the road for his political career. Some of us dream of being prime minister. But how many of us go for it?

Maryse Bertrand, like me, stuck it out, but in her retirement from active practice sits on the boards of a number of major corporations and, as mentioned, is serving as vice-chair of McGill University.

Walied Soliman evolved from young lawyer to self-developed expert in proxy battles and hostile takeover bids, and then into Canadian chair of Norton Rose Fulbright, a major international law firm.

André Bacchus heeded the little voice in the back of his head, abandoning a lucrative position as a third-year securities lawyer with a Manhattan firm to teach young lawyers and now law students how to develop their own careers. Each change has brought him unexpected challenges working with young people, which he finds enormously satisfying.

Alyssa Tomkins has stayed at private practice, moving from major law firm to litigation boutique. She benefited from the mentorship of two iconic litigators, east and west: Ron Caza in

Ottawa and Peter Gall in Vancouver. She observed their strengths: they were both incredibly persuasive, even when their cases were weak; were never afraid to advance a novel argument; and were bold in the face of resistance. She learned even more from their challenges: when to tell a client that their case has little chance of success, and when it's in their best interest to give up. She has also learned to separate empathy for the client's plight from the independent advisor's most important quality: objectivity.

Marc Le Blanc knew it was time to leave an IP litigation boutique when a television network offered a position in their legal department. He'd had enough of private practice. Had he not made that jump, the opportunity to build a team at TVO might not have presented itself.

Tim Hutzul would tell you that he is more like you than anyone I write about. He's worn so many different career hats, learned so many skills, and picked himself up after setbacks. All that has contributed to his versatility and excellent judgment, both critical assets in his current position as GC at Shawcor and in his pro bono work with Canada Basketball.

As you can see, there is no one-size-fits-all. The only points we all agree upon are the following:

1. Go with your gut.

2. Don't let fear dominate your decision making.

3. Prioritize what's important in your life and ask whether your work environment is consistent with those priorities.

4. You'll never know whether you'll be successful by guessing forward. Trust your instincts, build your skills, and judge yourself by the journey.

5. Set and reset your definition of success. It will change with experience.

6. Dare to have fun.

Conclusion

We're going to conclude with some recent industry findings compiled by Thomson Reuters Canada explaining the main reasons why almost half the general counsel surveyed in 2019 were in the process of switching law firms. It had nothing to do with the legal competency of the lawyers. It is also taken for granted that lawyers are keeping pace with technological advances to become more efficient.

Instead, the attributes the GCs most valued were as follows:

- Relationship management: the combination of being responsive, keeping one question ahead of the client, and creating a two-way street of setting, meeting, and measuring expectations.

- Communication, which they define as listening to the client so that you understand what is right for the particular client in their circumstances, rather than in theory.

- Entrepreneurial mindset intertwining law and business, and calling on agility, efficiency, adaptability, and keen problem-solving skills. These skills they rated as most critical and most rare.

Does any of this now sound familiar?

If you can follow the guiding principles laid out in this book, if you keep a line of communication open with your clients, if you take the time to learn their businesses, if you talk business to them rather than law, if you stop worrying about proving how much law you know and focus instead on how to apply it to client solutions, you will emerge at the top of your field.

Some final words of advice from the experts that will now make more sense to you:

"Great lawyers excel at three critical skills…Understand people, master technology, and as you develop, learn to empower those below you." — FERNANDO GARCIA

"More than anything else: don't let the fear of making a decision paralyze you." — ANDRÉ BACCHUS

"Make sure you do things you're not good at. That's how you get good." — MARYSE BERTRAND

"When choosing a firm to work at, don't focus so much on where they fit in on the 'bullseye' or ranking in magazines. Match yourself to a firm consistent with your values." — ERIN O'TOOLE

"The one fallacy holding you back: I'm too old to make a change." — LORENE NAGATA

"When I was at the cusp of partnership, I asked myself the toughest question of my life. Was private practice where I wanted to be?" — BEN WESTELMAN

"I wanted a firm with no rules, no management board, no strategic plan. So I built my own firm." — AARON FRIEWALD

"If you want to stay mentally strong, you must learn to separate your identity from your statistics." — RYAN MIDDLETON

"The law I learned practising wasn't nearly as important as the lessons from my mentors. Be ready for surprises. Try to think differently than everyone else." — ERIN O'TOOLE

"I was on track, but on track for what? For where? Not for where I needed to go." — ANDRÉ BACCHUS

"In career building, as in work, you need to know there are people you can rely on and who can rely on you." — JENNIFER POLLOCK, CPA

"Go with your gut. It's scary how effective that is." — CHRISTINA PORRETTA

"I am still learning the lesson that I am more than good enough, and that I don't have to measure it by my position, compensation, or recognition." — JENNIFER LEE

"Most of my clients first hired me as the expert who could advise on my area of expertise. Eventually, the ones who were evergreen, saw me as a business advisor, someone who could help talk through their problems and help chart the future of their businesses." — NORMAN BACAL

The final nail to hammer home is this: your career is entirely in your hands. Do not let anyone convince you otherwise. Keep an eye open for opportunity, don't be afraid to take risks, and realize that fear is the only thing holding you back from reaching your full potential.

For more books by Norman Bacal please check out my website: **Normanbacal.com**

Feel free to subscribe to my newsletter on my website, which will include how to get my upcoming sequel, *Triple F.*

Acknowledgements

To my readers, Tim Hutzul and Matt Diskin, who thoroughly reviewed every thought and provided much needed criticism and perspective, many thanks for your contributions to the final product. Thanks as well to Gary Luftspring, Justice Lorne Sossin, and Joseph Groia for their suggestions.

To my editor, Jennifer Glossop, thanks for your guidance in helping me give my original thoughts the right shape and direction. To my other editor, Marie-Lynn Hammond, thank you once again for your valuable suggestions.

About the Author

Norman Bacal founded the Toronto office of Heenan Blaikie in 1989, and went on to build and lead the law firm for fifteen years, as it became one of Canada's leading brands as a national enterprise with over 1100 employees. He was also among the world's leading entertainment attorneys representing studios like Warner Bros and MGM. He served on the board of directors of Lionsgate for almost ten years, while they were producing the Hunger Games.

In 2015 he retired from practice and since that time has been mentoring young professionals and speaking regularly at universities and to professional firms about career development and leadership. He is a frequent keynote speaker.

Manufactured by Amazon.ca
Bolton, ON

21493597R00111